THE VAULT CAREER GUIDE TO
Consultin on

is made possible through the generous support of the following sponsors:

BAIN & COMPANY

 Booz | Allen | Hamilton
delivering results that endure

INSEAD
The Business School
for the World

London Business School

MITCHELL MADISON GROUP
Global Management Consultants

OC&C Strategy Consultants

OLIVER WYMAN

Roland Berger
Strategy Consultants

Teach First
LEARNING TO LEAD

Teach First's graduate programme is a unique opportunity to be different and to make a difference. It's an innovative combination of teaching with management skills training and leadership development, plus unparalleled internship, networking and coaching opportunities.

Whatever you aim to do with your career, Teach First.

I taught first

www.teachfirst.org.uk

Teach **First**
LEARNING TO LEAD

Where do you
see yourself in

10 years?

5 years?

2 years?

MBA Programme

London Business School
Regent's Park
London NW1 4SA
Tel +44 (0)20 7000 7505
Fax +44 (0)20 7000 7501
Email mba1@london.edu
www.london.edu/mba/ambition/

It's the question we will all hear at least once in our career. With an MBA from London Business School, it is a question that has no limitations.

The London Business School MBA provides the skills, opportunities and global connections for you to achieve your career goals.

Our direct access to London's impressive finance and consulting recruiter base, excellent relationships with over 50 private equity firms and connections with 100 major corporations ensure you have the opportunities you need to satisfy your ambition.

Only the most talented are invited to attend our global classroom, for a learning experience that is both character forming and life changing.

Could this be you?

To download a brochure on our MBA programme visit www.london.edu/mba/ambition/

London experience. World impact.

You have one year to
challenge your thinking,
change your outlook and
choose your future.

INSEAD

The Business School
for the World

The MBA Programme
www.insead.edu/mba

THINKING TIME…

…IN THE BATH?

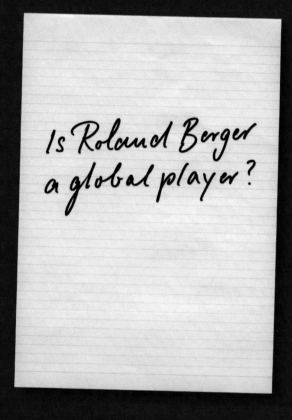

→ In the league in which we operate, there are no national consultancies anymore. For a long time now, Roland Berger has been an organization that is global through and through, with 33 offices in 23 countries. → More than 75 % of our projects involve challenges in the international arena. Three things are essential for meeting them: experience abroad, a cosmopolitan outlook and a team spirit that integrates diverse cultures and languages. → Are you intrigued by the opportunity of contributing these elements to a project? Are you ready to take on the world?

Roland Berger
Strategy Consultants

IT'S CHARACTER THAT CREATES IMPACT. WWW.ROLANDBERGER.COM

The media's watching Vault!
Here's a sampling of our coverage.

"[Vault tells] prospective joiners what they really want to know about the culture, the interview process, the salaries and the job prospects."
- *The Financial Times*

"Thanks to Vault, the truth about work is just a tap of your keyboard away."
- *The Telegraph*

"The best place on the Web to prepare for a job search."
– *Fortune*

"For those hoping to climb the ladder of success, [Vault's] insights are priceless."
– *Money* magazine

"A killer app."
– *The New York Times*

"To get the unvarnished scoop, check out Vault."
– *Smart Money* magazine

"Vault has a wealth of information about major employers and job-searching strategies as well as comments from workers about their experiences at specific companies."
– *The Washington Post*

CAREER GUIDE

VAULT CAREER GUIDE TO
CONSULTING

E U R O P E A N   E D I T I O N

CAREER
GUIDE

VAULT CAREER GUIDE TO

CONSULTING

E U R O P E A N   E D I T I O N

CONSULTING

By Eric Chung, Jim Slepicka, Philip Herrey,
Eduardo Junco and the staff of vault

Library of Congress CIP Data is available.

ISBN 13: 978-1-58131-515-8

ISBN 10: 1-58131-515-5

Printed in the United Kingdom

ACKNOWLEDGMENTS

Vault's acknowledgments:

We are extremely grateful to Vault's entire staff for all their help in the editorial, production and marketing processes. Vault also would like to acknowledge the support of our investors, clients, employees, family, and friends. Thank you!

Author acknowledgments:

Eric Chung thanks his wonderful new bride and muse, Laura, for being a constant source of joy and inspiration in everything he does.

Table of Contents

Visit **Vault Europe's Consulting Career Channel** at www.Vault.com/Europe for insider firm
profiles, employee surveys of consultants in Europe, job listings, expert consulting career
advice, insider salary information and more.   V∧ULT   CAREER LIBRARY   ix

Chapter 4: The Hiring Process   49

Chapter 5: The Interview   69

Visit **Vault Europe's Consulting Career Channel** at **www.Vault.com/Europe** for insider firm
profiles, employee surveys of consultants in Europe, job listings, expert consulting career
advice, insider salary information and more.   V/\ULT   CAREER
                                                                     LIBRARY   **xi**

Introduction

Your dream job?

Love the idea of jetting to locations both exotic and banal and getting paid very well for your intellectual capital? A lot of consultants (current and prospective) do, too.

Consulting continues to rank among the most popular professions for emerging graduates and those securing MBAs, and for good reason. As one of the best-paid professions for recent graduates, consulting offers lucrative salary packages and the chance to meet elite FTSE 100 or DAX30 managers. Consultants also work on some of the most interesting issues in business today: high-level strategy and integration issues.

But consulting careers are no walk in the park. Pressures are high; travel can be onerous; the interview process can be painful; many firms still have an up or out thinking and the risks of redundancy can be high in a difficult economic climate. Before setting off on the consulting route too enthusiastically, get a sense of how you might like it. Understand where the industry is going, your role in the industry, and how closely it fits with your needs and personality.

If you're reading this in an attempt to decide whether or not consulting is for you, we've got some advice. Do a personal inventory of your skills and talents, as well as your interests or what you merely enjoy. Also, find out about other professionals' experiences — both the war stories and the rewards. If your network doesn't include other consultants, use the message boards on Vault's consulting channel or join an industry organisation for leads. And read this guide to see if consulting really interests you.

Just remember that positions are limited, and competition ranks among the highest of many industries. Even if you have an INSEAD MBA or decades of experience, breaking into consulting and having a successful career requires perseverance and the sharpest of networking and persuasion skills. The potential rewards, however, are great.

Visit **Vault Europe's Consulting Career Channel** at **www.Vault.com/Europe** for insider firm profiles, employee surveys of consultants in Europe, job listings, expert consulting career advice, insider salary information and more.

VAULT CAREER LIBRARY

1

CAREER GUIDE

THE SCOOP

CONSULTING

The Basics of Consulting

CHAPTER 1

What is Consulting?

A giant industry, a moving target

Consulting, in the business context, means the giving of advice for fees. Consultants offer their advice and skill in solving problems, and are hired by companies who need the expertise and outside perspective that consultants possess. Some consulting firms specialise in giving advice on management and strategy, while others are known as technology specialists. Some concentrate on a specific industry area, like financial services or retail, and still others are more like gigantic one-stop shops with divisions that dispense advice on everything from top-level strategy, to choosing training software, to saving money on paper clips.

But consulting firms have one thing in common: they run on the power of their people. The only product consulting firms ultimately have to offer is their ability to make problems go away. As a consultant, you are that problem-solver.

Not the kind of consulting we mean

As a standalone term, "consulting" lacks real meaning. In a sense, everyone's a consultant. Have you ever been asked by a friend, "Do I look good in orange?" Then you've been consulted about your colour sense. There are thousands upon thousands of independent consultants who peddle their expertise and advice on everything from retrieving data from computers to cat astrology. There are also fashion consultants, image consultants, and wedding consultants. For the purposes of this career guide, we are going to use the term "consulting" to refer specifically to management consulting.

Management consulting firms sell business advisory services to the leaders of corporations, governments, and non-profit organisations. Typical concentrations in consulting include strategy, IT, HR, finance, and operations. Types of problems in consulting include pricing, marketing, new product strategy, IT implementation, or government policy. Finally, consulting firms sell services in virtually any industry, such as pharmaceuticals, fast moving consumer goods, or energy.

Firms can be organised or broken up according to topic, type of problem, or industry. For example, a firm might focus on strategy problems only, but in virtually any industry. Bain & Company is an example of one such firm. Another firm might focus on a specific industry, but advise on nearly any type of issue. Kurt Salmon Associates, which focuses on consumer goods and retail, is an example of this type of firm. Many of the larger firms have a "matrix" organisation with industry practice groups but also functional practice groups. And some firms are extremely specialised. For example, a firm might have only two employees, both focusing solely on competitive analysis in the telecommunications industry. All of these are examples of management consulting.

Caveats about consulting

All this might sound great, but before we go on, we should address some common misconceptions about consulting.

- **Implementation** – You might be thinking, "All consultants do is figure out problems at companies and explain them. Great! I'm going to be making great money for doing something really easy." Unfortunately, that's not true. Spotting a client's problems is a mere fraction of the battle. (Most people with a fair amount of common sense and an outsider's perspective can identify a client's problems. And in many cases, clients also understand where the problems lie.)

  The job of the consultant, therefore, isn't just about knowing what's wrong. It's about working out how to make it right. Even finding the solution isn't the end of the story. Consultants must make sure the solution isn't too expensive or impractical to implement. (Many consulting firms have what's called an 80 percent rule: It's better to put in place a solution that takes care of 80 percent of the problem than to strive for a perfect solution that can't be put into place.) A corollary to this is the 80/20 rule: 80 percent of a problem can be solved in 20 percent of the time. Consultants must also get "buy-in" from the clients. Not only does bureaucracy often make implementation tough, but consultants must also convince individual client employees to help them make solutions work. It's tough to solve problems — and that's why clients hire consultants.

- **Glamour** – Consulting can indeed be exciting and high profile, but this is the exception, not the rule. Chances are, you won't be sitting across from the Chief Executive at your next project kick-off, and you probably won't be staying in five-star hotels in the coolest cities in the world (though both are possible). Depending on the industry and location of your client's business, your environment might be a mid-range hotel in a small city,

VAULT CAREER LIBRARY

and you might be working with the director of one of the company's many business units.

• **Prestige** – Consulting is widely thought of as a prestigious career among business circles, particularly graduates with MBAs. However, outside these circles, consultants often have a bad image. Many employees of large organisations have seen young graduate consultants who earn far more than they ever will, come into their company with limited knowledge of their industry, create lots of havoc and change, and leave them to pick up the pieces. Positive press for consultants is rare. In contrast to work in investment banking, your work in consulting will probably never get mentioned in *The Financial Times*. Very few consulting firms are publicly recognised for the help they give.

As a result, few people outside of the industry really understand what consulting is. In fact, a running joke about consulting is that no one can explain it, no matter how hard or many times one tries. If you want a job you can explain to your grandmother, consulting isn't for you. Most "civilians" won't have heard of your firm — unless it has been involved in a scandal, that is.

• **Income** – The salary looks attractive on paper, but remember, it's not easy money. Divide your salary over the (often large) number of hours, and the pay per hour isn't much better than other business careers.

So what does a consultant actually do, anyway?

Most "non-consultants" are mystified by the actual job and its day-to-day responsibilities. There are good reasons why this is. While you're used to giving advice and solving problems, you may not understand how this translates into a career path. The problem is compounded because consultants tend to use a very distinctive vocabulary. You may not know what your skill set is, or how not to boil the ocean, or what the heck consultants mean when they talk about helicopering. In addition, many consulting firms have their own specific philosophies and problem-attacking frameworks, which only raise the level of jargon. (If you're stumped, check out the glossary at the end of this book.)

The short answer is that you will be working on projects of varying lengths at varying sites for different clients. What you do will depend on your seniority, experience, phase of the project and your company. If you are a partner, you are selling work most of the time, whereas if you have a recent MBA degree, you are probably overseeing a couple of entry-level consultants doing research. For the most part, we'll describe the job that entry-level and mid-level (MBA

Visit **Vault Europe's Consulting Career Channel** at www.Vault.com/Europe for insider firm profiles, employee surveys of consultants in Europe, job listings, expert consulting career advice, insider salary information and more.

VAULT CAREER LIBRARY

7

or the equivalent) consultants do. Generally, projects follow the pitching/research/analysis/report writing cycle.

Depending where you are in the project lifecycle, here are some of the things you could be doing:

Pitching – Selling the practice

- Helping to sell and market the firm (preparing documents and researching prospective clients in preparation for sales calls)

- Helping to write the proposal

- Presenting a sales pitch to a prospective client (usually with PowerPoint, Microsoft's presentation software)

Research

- Performing secondary research on the client and its industry using investment banking reports and other research sources (these include Bloomberg, Factiva, Hoover's Online, Mintel and Companies House filings but also extensive 'googling')

- Interviewing the client's customers to gather viewpoints on the company

- Checking your firm's data banks for previous studies that it has done in the industry or with the client, and speaking to the project leads about their insights on the firm

- Facilitating a weekly client team discussion about the client company's business issues

Analysis

- Building Excel discounted cash flow (DCF) and/or other quantitative financial models

- Analysing the gathered data and the model for insights

- Helping to generate recommendations

Reporting

- Preparing the final presentation (typically a "deck" of PowerPoint slides, though some firms write up longer reports in Microsoft Word format)

- Helping to present the findings and recommendations to the client

Implementation

- Acting as a project manager for the implementation of your strategy, if your firm is typically active during the implementation phase of a project

- Executing the coding, systems integration, and testing of the recommended system, if you work for an IT consulting practice

- Documenting the team's work after the project is over

Administration

- Working on internal company research when your firm has no projects for you. (Being unstaffed is referred to as being "on the beach," a pleasant name for what is often a tedious time.)

- Filling out weekly time tracking and expense reports

Keep in mind that the assessment phase — usually the most interesting part — is probably the shortest part of any assignment. Consultants staffed on projects typically do a lot of research, financial analysis, Excel model building and presentation. You will attend lots of meetings in your quest to find the data, create the process and meet the people who will help you resolve the issues you've been hired to address. And, when you're not staffed, you will spend time "on the beach" doing research on prospective clients and helping with marketing efforts. (It's called "on the beach" because the time when you're not staffed on a paid engagement is usually less frenetic – though not always so!) Consulting firms spend a lot of time acquiring the work, and depending on how the firm is structured or how the economy is doing, you could spend significant amounts of time working on proposals. For you, this usually means lots of research, which is then elucidated on the omnipresent PowerPoint slides.

To some extent, though, the boundaries of the job are virtually limitless. Each project carries with it a new task, a new spreadsheet configuration, a new type of sales conference, or an entirely new way of thinking about business. To top it all off, you often must travel to your work assignment and work long hours in a pressurised environment. It's not easy.

Visit **Vault Europe's Consulting Career Channel** at www.Vault.com/Europe for insider firm profiles, employee surveys of consultants in Europe, job listings, expert consulting career advice, insider salary information and more.

V/\ULT   CAREER LIBRARY   9

Consulting Skill Sets

Consultants focus their energies in a wide variety of practice areas and industries. Their individual jobs, from a macro level, are as different as one could imagine. While a supply chain consultant advises a client about lead times in their production facility, another consultant is creating a training protocol for a new software package. What could be more different?

Despite the big picture differences, however, consultants' day-to-day skill sets are, by necessity, very similar. (Before we go any further: by skill set, we mean "your desirable attributes and skills that contribute value as a consultant.")

Before we talk about the skill sets, keep in mind that there is a big difference between the job now and the job six to eight years from now, if and when you are a partner. We are going to talk about whether you would like the job now, but you should think about whether this might be a good long-term career for you. Is your goal to see it through to partner? If you would rather have an interesting job for six years, you just have to know you have the qualities to be a good consultant and manager. To be a partner, you have to be a persuasive salesperson. You will spend nearly 100 percent of your time selling expensive services to companies who don't think they need help. Your pay and job security will depend on your ability to make those sales.

Do you have the following characteristics in your skill set?

• Do you work well in teams? Consultants don't work alone. Not only do they frequently brainstorm with other consultants, but they also often work with employees at the client company, or even with consultants from other companies hired by the client. Consultants also frequently attend meetings and interview potential information sources. If you're the sort of person who prefers to work alone in quiet environments, you will not enjoy being a consultant.

• Do you multi-task well? Not only can consulting assignments be frenetic, but consultants are often staffed on more than one assignment meaning that you will need to divide your time and effort among a multitude of tasks within these. Superior organisational skills and a good sense of prioritisation are your friends. Would your friends describe you as a really busy person who's involved in a ton of activities, and still able to keep your personal life on track?

- Speaking of friends, do you like talking to people? Do you find yourself getting into interesting conversations over lunch and dinner? If you consider yourself a true introvert and find that speaking to people all day saps your energy, you will probably find consulting enervating. While on the road, many of the meals and social occasions will involve client contact (some refer to this part of consulting as client bonding) and will require you to wear your best smile and engage in conversations. On the other hand, if you truly relish meetings, talking to experts, explaining your viewpoints, cajoling others to cooperate with you and making impromptu presentations, you've got some valuable talents in your consulting skill set.

- Did you love school? Did you really like going to class and doing your homework? There's a high correlation between academic curiosity and enjoyment of consulting.

- Are you comfortable with math? Consulting firms don't expect you to be a math professor, but you should be comfortable with figures, as well as commonly used programs like Excel, Access and PowerPoint. If you hate math, you will hate consulting. On a related note, you should also relish and be good at analysis and thinking creatively. Consultants have a term, now infiltrating popular culture, called "out of the box thinking." This means the ability to find solutions that are "outside the box" – not constrained by commonly accepted facts.

- Are you willing to work 70, even 80 hours a week? Consultants must fulfil client expectations. If you must work 80 hours a week to meet client expectations, then that will be your fate. If you have commitments outside work, for example, you may find consulting hours difficult. Even if you have no major commitments outside work, understand what such a schedule means to you. Try working from 8 a.m. to 10 p.m. one day. Now imagine doing so five days a week for months on end. While consultancies attempt to accommodate the working hours to be flexible, the pressure remains high, and particularly as deadlines approach, you should expect to work well beyond the normal working hours.

- Last, but certainly not least, are you willing to travel frequently? (See the next section for a discussion of travel in consulting.)

Be truthful. If you can't answer most of these points with a resounding "yes," consulting is most likely not for you. The point is not just to get the job, but also to know what you're getting into — and to truly want to be a consultant.

Visit **Vault Europe's Consulting Career Channel** at **www.Vault.com/Europe** for insider firm profiles, employee surveys of consultants in Europe, job listings, expert consulting career advice, insider salary information and more.

VAULT CAREER LIBRARY 11

The Traveling Salesman Problem

A lot of people go into the consulting field with the notion that travel is fun. "Travelling four days a week? No problem! My last holiday to Italy was a blast!" However, many soon find the travelling consultant's life to be a nightmare. Many consultants leave the field solely because of travel requirements.

Here's what we mean by consulting travel. Different consulting firms have different travel models, but there are two basic ones:

• A number of consulting firms (the larger ones) spend four days on the client site. This means traveling to the destination city Monday morning, spending three nights in a hotel near the client site, and flying home late Thursday night. (This will, of course, vary, depending on client preference and flight times.) The same firms often try to staff "regionally" to reduce flying time for consultants.

• The other popular travel model is to go to the client site "as needed." This generally means traveling at the beginning of the project for a few days, at the end of the project for the presentation, and a couple of times during the project. There is less regularity and predictability with this travel model, but there is also less overall time on the road.

Here are some variations of these travel modes that pop up frequently:

• International projects involve a longer-term stay on the client site. (Flying consultants to and from the home country every week can get expensive.) For example, the consultant might stay two or three weeks on or near the client site (the client might put you up in a corporate apartment instead of a hotel to save costs) and then go home for a week, repeating the process until the end of the project.

Many of the companies you will deal with as a consultant will have offices in a number of European cities. While your work will usually involve a reference person within the corporate head office you will have to deal with people across a variety of countries and cultures which can be exciting in some cases but also tiring and tedious.

• Then, there is the "local" project that is really a long commute into a suburb, sometimes involving up to two hours in a car. While most big consultancies are based right in the centre of London, you'll hardly find any industrial clients within the M25 perimeter. If you are working for BP in Sunbury or for BT in Kings Langley you might opt to stay at a local hotel after working late, instead of taking the long drive home. This is not very different from non-local travel, and it can be more grueling, due to the car commute.

You need to ask yourself a number of questions to see if you are travel-phobic. For example, when you pack to go on holiday, do you stress about it? Do you always underpack or overpack? Do you hate flying or taking trains several times per week? Do you hate to drive? Do you mind sleeping in hotel rooms for long periods of time? Are you comfortable with the idea of travelling to remote towns and staying there for three or four nights every week for ten weeks? Do you mind being away from your other half (and children if you have them) for up to three nights a week? Does your family mind? Will your spouse understand and not hold it against you if you have to cancel your anniversary dinner because the client wants you to stay a day later? If you and your spouse both travel for work, who will take care of the pets? Does the idea of managing your weekly finances and to-do lists from the road bother you?

If these questions make your stomach churn, look for consulting companies that promise a more stable work environment. For example, if you work in financial consulting and live in London, most of your clients may be local. But because consulting firms don't always have the luxury of choosing their clients, they can't guarantee that you won't travel. Moreover, many large companies build their corporate campus where they can find cost-effective space, often in the suburbs or large corporate parks. (If you absolutely can not travel, some of the largest consulting firms, such as Accenture, have certain business units that can guarantee a non-traveling schedule. Ask.)

Note that travel is common in the consulting field, but not all consultants travel. And not all clients expect you to be on site all the time. It absolutely depends on the firm's travel model, industry, your location, and most importantly, your project.

Do not think of work travel as possibly like your last vacation. Consulting firms and clients are demanding and will require you to travel back and forth with little slack time and work long hours while on site at the client's. Only if you're lucky will there be some time left to sample the local restaurants with your team.

But not all is bad. Some consultancies are happy to arrange your flights in a manner that is a win-win for all parties. If you are travelling to Lisbon on Monday morning, why not book your flight for the previous Saturday and make a weekend out of it?

Visit **Vault Europe's Consulting Career Channel** at www.Vault.com/Europe for insider firm profiles, employee surveys of consultants in Europe, job listings, expert consulting career advice, insider salary information and more.

VAULT CAREER LIBRARY 13

Who Hires Consultants, and Why?

Companies, governments, and non-profit institutions hire consultants for a number of reasons. Every consulting project springs from a client's need for help, or at least the kind of help that short-term, internal employment can't solve. Some clients, for example, need to overhaul their entire IT infrastructure, yet they're out of touch with the latest back-end systems or don't have the staff resources for such a large project. Other clients may be merging, but lack any experience with post-merger staffing procedures, and need a neutral party to mediate. Some clients may need an outsider's perspective on a factory shutdown. Perhaps a client wants to bring in extra industry knowledge. And in a recession, some clients are bringing in consultants with turnaround expertise, because they lack the deep experience with financial and corporate restructuring that such experts can supply.

Consultants get hired for political reasons too. Launching big projects can be very cumbersome, particularly at FTSE 100 companies. In order for a single pound to be spent on such a project, most companies require board level approval. And without a major consultancy's brand name attached to the project, approval can be hard to get. But once a consulting firm steps into the picture, everyone involved has plausible deniability in the event that the project fails. There is an old adage: "No one ever got fired for hiring McKinsey" (or a similarly prestigious consulting firm.) Some clients still adhere to this as a rule of thumb.

Second, even if a giant project gets the green light, there's no guaranteeing it will be implemented. The reason? Simple bureaucratic inertia. Senior executives lose interest. Sponsors move on to other issues. In short, companies lose their focus. By bringing in consultants to oversee large projects, companies ensure that someone is always watching the ball. In many cases, the correct solution may be quite evident to many, but having it confirmed by an outside party makes implementing a plan easier politically.

Consultants have another political use. Companies with an itch to fire a percentage of their workforce often like to bring in consultants. When the consultants recommend a workforce reduction, the company can fire at will, blaming their hired guns for the downsizing.

For some types of consulting (particularly outsourcing or IT), consultants are actually a form of cost-effective labour. It costs the firm less money to hire some outsiders to help them with a project, rather than employ some folks full-time at the expense of a competitive salary and benefits package. Consultants may also get the job done faster, not because they are necessarily better, but because the company might not get away with forcing regular employees to adhere to a compressed time frame by staying late. By definition, consultants are hired to work not at the pace of the corporation but at a differently prescribed pace. A contingency performance basis makes this an even better deal for the client.

Whatever the reasons for hiring consultants, they're bound to be compelling — because, even despite the cost-effectiveness argument in some cases, consultants are very costly on average. Given travel expenses, hotel bills, and actual project fees, prices for consultants can easily climb into the £300 per hour range.

The worker behind the curtain

Consultants are a back-room breed of professional. In joint projects with their clients, they do much of the work and can expect none of the recognition. All consultants must deliver bottom-line value, and often spend countless hours huddled in cramped spaces to do just that. If you do a great job, chances are your client will thank you, but you may never hear about it again. In some cases, you will leave your project before its completion and may never know whether it succeeded or failed.

If you enjoy recognition and completion, you will want to consider the type of consulting firm you join. Does your firm have a history of repeat business? If so, you will have a better chance of seeing the client through different projects and business cycles; you may even work with the same client on different engagements. (Mars & Co., for example, is known for its deep and lasting relationships with clients.) Other firms might offer a methodology that isn't as repeatable. If your firm focuses solely on competitive analysis studies, chances are that if your client stays in the same industry, you won't need to sell that service to them again.

Economic consulting firms often help law firms with litigation support, including research, economic analysis, and testimonies. This can be very interesting work, and since you're supporting one side or the other of a public dispute, you will certainly know how the fruits of your labour will turn out. Depending on the size of the dispute, so might everyone else who follows the business news.

Another example is M&A consulting. Some firms, like L.E.K. Consulting, have practice areas specifically focused on due diligence, company analysis, and transaction support. On the positive side, this type of consulting will give you insights into a wide variety of industries and companies. The bad news is that on such projects, you are subject to the even longer and more erratic hours suffered by other M&A professionals. On the bright side, you will eventually read in The Financial Times about any triumph enjoyed by your client.

Visit **Vault Europe's Consulting Career Channel** at www.Vault.com/Europe for insider firm profiles, employee surveys of consultants in Europe, job listings, expert consulting career advice, insider salary information and more.

VAULT CAREER LIBRARY **15**

Your firm may not be mentioned, but at least you will be able to see the results of your hard work become a reality. (It'll also be easier for you to transition to other financial work in the future, if that is your wish.)

So, think about the level of recognition and completion you need for your work, and look for a firm that does the type of work that suits that level. If you find that you require higher levels of recognition and completion than any type of consulting can offer, then you may want to look into other professions.

Commercial Due Diligence (CDD)

Mergers and acquisitions in the corporate world bring with them a large amount of paperwork and a large number of legal and required documents. These documents will give the reader a full overview of the company's position, structure, financials, legal and tax situation. The commercial due diligence serves the purpose of assessing the industry the company operates in and the position of the company within this industry. The CDD has long been regarded by many as a secondary document but has continually increased in importance as buyers, banks and investors have acknowledged the importance of an independent opinion on market performance and company position.

In recent years the number of mergers and acquisitions worldwide has soared, driven by low interest rates and the dawn of private equity groups. Many consultancies have recognised this as an important source of revenues and have tackled the market full on. Commercial due diligence work requires consultancies to act differently than they usually do as the work normally needs to be carried out under strict non-disclosure agreements and immense time pressure. London, as one of the world's foremost financial centres and certainly Europe's investment banking capital, has experienced a solid boom in this commercial due diligence service with a number of dedicated consultancies and separate departments within the larger consulting houses addressing this market exclusively. Commercial due diligences are less commonplace in other European countries but are expected to play an increasing role as the process becomes standard in every transaction. If you have a natural interest and curiosity in a broad range of subjects, products and services and are able to acquire and process information quickly and critically, then this might be a type of work that you might be interested in. But be aware that mergers and acquisitions activity undergoes considerable cyclical fluctuation, making this line of work more risky.

A Consultant Among Accountants

The 'Big Four' accounting houses (Price Waterhouse Coopers, KPMG, Ernst & Young and Deloitte) recently started tapping into the market for commercial due diligence. These large business service houses already lead the way in providing legal, tax and financial due diligence services and have sought to fill the gap in the offering by adding the commercial assessment to the package, hence capturing all the fees available during a transaction. This has meant that considerable effort has been made towards hiring consultants to address this need and all of the 'Big Four' now include sizeable consulting and commercial practices boasting 20-50 consultants.

Industry History and Data Points

A brief history of consulting

People have traded wisdom for pay since the dawn of time. Nonetheless, consulting as big business only came into being around the start of the 20th century.

The first consultants drew from their engineering backgrounds to conduct projects for their clients. The now-bankrupt Arthur D. Little is widely recognised as the first such firm, founded in 1886 in Cambridge, Massachusetts. Booz Allen Hamilton was established in the early 20th century with a similar structure.

The trend continued when James "Mac" McKinsey, a University of Chicago professor, established his "accounting and engineering advisors" firm in 1926, offering a proposition similar to consulting. Over time, he developed a unique, integrated approach for his clients, which he called his "General Survey." Instead of hiring traditional engineers, he recruited experienced executives and trained them in a framework of analysis. The new approach considered goals, strategies, policies, organization, facilities, procedures, and personnel. In the late 1950s, a number of other consulting firms emerged with focused strategies and novel frameworks.

The most notable innovator, the Boston Consulting Group (BCG), developed the experience curve. The experience curve proposed that declines in most industries were directly correlated to cost as a function of cumulative experience. BCG later extended its original concept by developing the growth share matrix, a tool that assesses a company's attractiveness within an industry. These frameworks are still used today by consultants in

Visit **Vault Europe's Consulting Career Channel** at www.Vault.com/Europe for insider firm profiles, employee surveys of consultants in Europe, job listings, expert consulting career advice, insider salary information and more.

V/\ULT   CAREER LIBRARY   17

order to understand business problems and opportunities. They are also used in case interviews, business analysis questions commonly given to prospective consultants. (More about cases later.)

Current Trends

Consultants and their clients are in a state of constant change. The typical client now requires more sophistication from its consultants' in-house skills and is more demanding in its requirements. For example, some clients now possess in-house strategy groups and have clear ideas of what their business means and the direction in which to head. This increased sophistication has led to a number of new developments in the industry, which in turn will impact your decision to enter the industry.

Specialisation

Until recently, the conventional wisdom at firms like McKinsey was to develop generalists who applied their learning across industries and geographies. That strategy is evolving. Clients increasingly demand that consultants come in with prior knowledge of their industry. While most of the larger firms still employ generalists, they now ask consultants to specialise earlier in their careers, often only two or three years after starting at the company. They sometimes also take on industry experts who might follow different (and possibly accelerated) career tracks than typical consultants.

Outside of the large consulting firms, more boutique consultancies are springing up. These boutiques have as few as two or three employees (and as many as 150 or so) and offer highly specialised expertise, for example consulting to the telecom industries, or providing expertise in marketing. Some of these firms are created by laid-off consultants or by those disaffected by recent mergers.

Industry acceptance of the boutiques has increased significantly. Particularly in the UK, boards of directors no longer insist on the McKinsey rubber stamp for their decisions. To the contrary, in the current cost-conscious environment, many large companies have put a blanket ban on consulting spend — the smaller specialists with their comparatively low fees often have a good chance of gaining an exception to these bans.

Implementation

Many clients no longer want to pay for mere strategic musing. Hence, many strategic consulting firms now stay on to ensure implementation of their recommendations. That is, clients want the strategic recommendation to contain an implementation plan — a roadmap to put the strategy into play — and they often want the consultants to be available for the implementation, at the very least by phone and more often on a part-time basis on the client site.

Of course, differences prevail. Strategy consultants lack powerhouse information technology skills, and systems players have a hard time convincing clients they can think "outside the box." But the success of strategy/systems hybrids like Booz Allen Hamilton suggests that convergence adds a successful competitive advantage — which means more competition for all consulting firms. Web consultancies have had an especially difficult time in convincing clients that they have the same implementation capabilities (or even the same strategic skills) as larger and more established competitors, as evidenced by the bankruptcy declarations of web consulting firms like Scient.

Cyclical nature

Consultants like to estimate future revenues for other industries. As a result, speculation abounds about the consulting industry's own revenues. In the late 1990s, aggressive penetration of emerging markets by companies (where consultants assess new markets) and rapid changes in client industries (privatisation, IT changes, and globalisation) were responsible for the marked growth in consulting.

But as the ultimate service industry, consulting depends heavily on the prospects of large corporations. Though global recessions create many issues for consultants to address, companies tend to cut outside costs (including consultants) when budgets are lean, which makes consulting companies vulnerable to layoffs and cost cutting.

The rough economy of 2001-2002 was not kind to consulting firms. Growth among the 50 largest firms, after exceeding 20 percent per year in the late 1990s, slumped to a piddling 2 percent in 2001, according to Kennedy Information's Consulting News. Now, the consulting industry is once again revving its engines. The last year has seen the strongest growth of revenues since the dot-com years. The 2005/6 consulting industry report (published by the UK Management Consultancies Association) shows that consulting has grown by 18% year on year amongst member firms — with pure management consulting growing by 40%. As a result, the number of employees in the consulting sector has grown by 27% in 2005/6. And growth is expected to continue along similar levels with other

Visit **Vault Europe's Consulting Career Channel** at **www.Vault.com/Europe** for insider firm profiles, employee surveys of consultants in Europe, job listings, expert consulting career advice, insider salary information and more.

VAULT CAREER LIBRARY

19

European markets reporting similar growth rates. Much of this growth is underpinned by increasing M&A activity which drives the need for restructuring, due diligence and post-merger integration (PMI) type projects.

Consulting across Europe

The UK and Germany are considered the most mature consulting markets in Europe. In terms of percentage of GDP spent on consulting, they are followed by Spain, Denmark and Portugal. In these terms, the least developed consulting markets in Western Europe are Greece, Italy and France. (2005 data from the Federation of European mangagement consulting associations, FEACO.)

Get them off me!

Around 2000, the Big Five consulting firms went through a period of striking out on their own — or, in several cases, joining forces with other companies. Because of increased scrutiny into the relationship between accounting and consulting services, led by the SEC in the United States, four of the Big Five firms sold or spun off their consulting arms in order to sever them from their accounting concerns.

Presciently, Ernst & Young sold its consulting unit to Cap Gemini in February 2000, creating Cap Gemini Ernst & Young now simply Gapgemini). KPMG Consulting was spun off from KPMG LLP in 2000 as well, renaming itself BearingPoint. PricewaterhouseCoopers is perhaps the most interesting of the five — just weeks after announcing an IPO and rebranding itself Monday (to the mirth of those who associate Mondays with drudgery), the firm announced it would be acquired by IBM in July 2002. Arthur Andersen Business Consulting, while not implicated in the Enron scandal (for those of you who shun all media outlets, accounting firm Arthur Andersen, owner of AABC, was mortally wounded as a result of its entanglement with the creative accounting at client energy firm Enron), has suffered the consequences of its association with Arthur Andersen. In the UK, its remaining partners and staff joined Deloitte, while in the US, some elements were also acquired by KPMG Consulting. Deloitte Consulting also announced a management buyout in 2002 but then aborted this move at the eleventh hour and distinctively pursued a strategy to integrate its consulting business more closely with other services such as corporate finance, audit and tax advice.

Today, all the remaining Big Four professional service firms, PWC, KPMG, Ernst & Young, and Deloitte, are re-establishing consulting practices as their non-compete agreements with the consultancies they spun off have expired. However, except for

Deloitte, the focus of the consulting arms of the Big Four relates to transaction services, performing due diligence assessments for potential mergers and acquisitions.

Victims of the economy

In the 1990s, consulting firms extended lots of offers and competed for the best candidates. Many of them, in hindsight, understand that they overhired (a euphemism often employed for this sad fact is "hired ahead of the curve"). A few years ago, consulting firms began to drastically scale back recruiting. Reviews have been more frequent and a lot harsher; in fact, many former consultants feel like they were unfairly "counselled out" of their positions through an "up-or-out" review process.

"Up-or-out" refers to the practice of requiring employees to advance their careers to the next level of responsibility or move out of the firm. Employees are informed whether they are up to firm standards when getting performance reviews. In the standard model, employees are warned that if they don't improve their performance by a certain date, they will be asked to resign from the firm. An employee and his or her manager agree upon a set of benchmarks by which they will measure performance improvements. The employee is usually not fired outright. Instead, he or she is asked to resign. (As noted, this extracted resignation can also be called "counselling out.") At its most basic, up-or-out is no more than the manifestation of a strong meritocracy.

With increasing demand, consultancies are cranking up the recruitment engine again. However, this time around, growth seems to be more carefully handled, with companies starting to hire only once current employees are overstretched. In addition, most firms still employ some version of the up-or-out policy because they have "pyramid" organisational schemes. This means that a firm has relatively more employees at the junior levels, with the partner level being the smallest and the analyst level being the largest group of employees. Up-or-out exists simply because consulting firms need some method of filtering out employees as they rise through the ranks.

Pay for performance

Some clients are now insisting that consulting firms accept pay for performance plans, termed "sweat equity" or "revenue sharing." Some consulting firms have done this for some time, while others have recently had to consider doing so. This is a change from the hourly or daily billing typical among consulting firms. It also means that consultants working on such projects are often pressed to work very long hours to meet the client's timetable.

Visit **Vault Europe's Consulting Career Channel** at **www.Vault.com/Europe** for insider firm profiles, employee surveys of consultants in Europe, job listings, expert consulting career advice, insider salary information and more.

VAULT CAREER LIBRARY   **21**

Consultancies that are providing market assessment ("due diligence") services for the private equity industry have sometimes adopted a variation of this practice. They agree to settle for a lower fee if the deal doesn't go through in return for receiving a premium for successful deals. This practice works mainly to the advantage of the private equity client as a risk mitigation measure. If you are considering applying for a consulting job with a consultancy that has adopted this form of compensation, be sure to ask about their success rate. Smaller, or more desperate, consultancies who agree to work on less probable deals may be doubly hit by this practice; on the one hand, they lose out on fees, on the other, they get fewer opportunities to work on lucrative post merger integration (PMI) projects.

Business Process Outsourcing: reliable, but no golden goose

The number of clients willing to pay for elaborate strategic projects is dwindling — but consulting firms need to keep revenue high. Public firms also need to show consistent revenue growth, lest their stock tank. One specialty that offers the possibility of this revenue growth is Business Process Outsourcing, or BPO.

BPO is the practice of outsourcing a non-core capability — for example, human resources services, call centres, treasury services, or training employees how to use Access. Consulting firms determine what needs to be outsourced in a company, locate the appropriate providers and manage the process for clients. Accenture is an example of a firm that launched a major business endeavour into outsourcing. (For those of you enthralled by consulting history, the Mitchell Madison Group, a McKinsey offshoot, made its name in BPO before being acquired by USWeb/CKS in June 1999. Web consultancy USWeb/CKS rebranded itself as MarchFIRST but subsequently went out of business in 2001.)

BPO is a growth field, but it's not a particularly profitable field. It's a service line that doesn't offer as much room for differentiation, meaning more competition for BPO clients and lower profits. Furthermore, consultants tend to find BPO assignments tedious.

Consulting Versus Other Business Careers

Consulting is just one of many desirable careers. Especially if you are at the undergraduate level, you are probably considering three or four other professions at the same time, including graduate work. We touch on a couple of these briefly for some reference, but we strongly encourage you to research them to a much greater extent on your own.

Investment banking

A lot of undergraduates and MBAs ask the "consulting or banking?" question. There are similarities between the two careers — including the high pay, long hours, and client focus — but the two tracks are very different.

It is very difficult to describe investment banking in a paragraph or two, but we'll take a shot at it anyway. In short, investment banks help companies raise money. Companies need money (capital) to grow their businesses, and investment banks sell securities (stocks or bonds) to public investors in order to generate these funds. Investment banks might also help a company to merge its assets with that of another company, manage and invest the money of wealthy individuals or institutions, or buy and sell securities to make money for itself.

One advantage of investment banking over consulting is pay. New analysts can make £40,000 to £50,000 in their first year, while MBA-level investment bankers can make £100,000 to £150,000 in total compensation for their first year. Bonuses often sweeten the pot. Another very attractive feature of investment banking is that the work is very high profile. Since all of the deals become public, the work your team does will make the Financial Times and other publications. For example, if you work for Merrill Lynch and you help TechCo go public, you might read in the newspaper how Merrill Lynch was the "lead underwriter" for TechCo's IPO. Investment banking suits the deal-driven person, the one who works off adrenalin and gets a personal thrill out of chasing and closing a deal. Banking is more heavily quantitative on a regular basis than consulting, though quantitative skills are important for both fields.

The biggest disadvantage is that on average, the hours in investment banking (especially at the junior levels) can be very long. How long? Try 100 hours a week as a realistic possibility. That means working 15 to 18 hours a day and frequent all-nighters. The hours are also less predictable than those of consulting, in general. Deals close or change at a moment's notice. The work tends to be much less flexible for employees with special scheduling needs — parents, for example. On the bright side, investment banking careers require less travel.

Industry

Corporate positions, like those at Shell, Procter & Gamble, or in high street banks, are another option. Many of them offer rotational programs to undergraduates and MBAs, where the new employee spends three to six months in a certain business unit before

Visit **Vault Europe's Consulting Career Channel** at **www.Vault.com/Europe** for insider firm profiles, employee surveys of consultants in Europe, job listings, expert consulting career advice, insider salary information and more.

VAULT CAREER LIBRARY 23

moving onto another one. At the end of 18 to 24 months, the employee typically chooses a business unit and stays there.

Industry historically has better job security, less travel, and shorter hours in exchange for less pay and, often, crushing bureaucracy. Flexibility and diversity is pegged strongly to individual corporate culture — some are terrific, others terrible. Corporations also represent your best opportunity if you are interested in marketing. The work can be just as compelling as consulting, with the key difference that you will be able see the strategies being put into action. And while you might make less money, you'll be in your own bed every night, and possibly even at a reasonable time

Graduate work

Some people suggest that working for a few years before returning for a masters is a smart idea. This can make a lot of sense if you are considering medical, law, or business school. If you're looking at MBA programmes, you should get some work experience prior to business school, as top MBA programmes admit very few candidates each year who have not had any full-time work experience. While fewer people work before going into law or studying medicine, it's still a smart idea — you'll gain business knowledge and perhaps save some money for the long, impoverished university days ahead.

You might also be considering entering a masters or PhD programme versus entering the consulting field. If you are most interested in teaching and research in a certain field, then perhaps a PhD is the way to go. You will enjoy an environment that is intellectually exciting. It can be a long road to the degree and professorship, however, and there are no guarantees of a chair.

Consulting Categories

The types of consulting that firms offer can be divided into four general categories: strategy, operations, information technology, and human resources. Strategy consulting accounts for about 23% of the European management consulting market, Operations for 40%, IT for 22% and HR consulting for 15%. A special category is boutique consulting, which reflects size (small) and focus (narrow). These categories often overlap, and most consulting firms offer multiple areas of consulting. Clients can now hire one firm, not several, to formulate overall strategy, review operational efficiency, and implement technology solutions.

European Consultancy Market

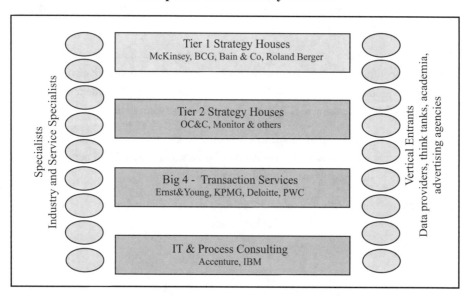

The figure above shows a conceptual view of the consulting market in Europe, and the clear tiering system in the consulting world.

Tier 1 comprises the classic names of consulting, the companies that have always been in the business and often blaze the trail for others to follow. McKinsey & Company, Bain & Company and The Boston Consulting Group are the groups with the highest visibility and longest history. Few European consultancies have managed to compete with their

Visit **Vault Europe's Consulting Career Channel** at www.Vault.com/Europe for insider firm profiles, employee surveys of consultants in Europe, job listings, expert consulting career advice, insider salary information and more.

VAULT CAREER LIBRARY   25

American counterparts. Roland Berger is a notable exception, having built a strong reputation across Europe and Asia from its German base.

Tier 2 includes a larger number of consultancies that have grown beyond their boutique status to cover a larger spectrum of customer needs moving beyond their core competence. OC&C and Monitor are good examples of this tier, moving beyond their respective retail and marketing core competence and now offering a broader range of services. Not only the boutique consultancies and Tier 1 spin-offs are posing a competitive threat to the strategy establishment; market research houses are also increasingly looking to amplify their services by offering strategy advice. Datamonitor, TNS (Taylor Nelson Sofres), IMS Health and AC Nielsen have all been trying to break into the strategy arena. However, so far most of these firms have struggled to convince industry that "thinking outside the box" is indeed a natural extension to ticking the boxes on surveys.

The Big Four, Ernst&Young, PriceWaterhouseCoopers, Deloitte and KPMG have a limited take on consulting, as past conflicts of interest have made them careful when offering their services outside the transaction services.

IT and process consultancies are project management specialists that advise on the solution of process or information problems as well as project manage and deliver the solution. Accenture is probably the most prolific company in this tier, with considerable scale and brand image, but IBM are increasingly making a name for themselves in IT consulting.

Specialists are an odd group of companies with little cohesion. Some may specialise in one limited subject matter (i.e. beverages or cars) and others may only fulfill a certain role (i.e. procurement consulting or consumer profit pool analysis).

Vertical entrants are all those that build on their expertise in a certain field to conduct consultancy work to those in need of subject experts.

Strategy Consulting

Strategy consulting aims to help a client's senior executives (for instance, the Chief Executive and board of directors) understand and face the strategic challenges of running their company or organisation. Strategy consultants work with the client's most senior management, since senior management sets a company's strategy and long-term plans.

Historically, strategy consulting firms made their recommendations, presented a "deck" (a report detailing the issues and recommendations), and walked away. Increasingly, however, clients expect strategists to stick around and implement their suggestions. Consequently, more consulting firms now tout their implementation capabilities.

Examples of typical strategy consulting engagements:

- Analysing why a clothing retailer generates lower sales per square foot than its competitors

- Understanding why West End theatres keep losing money and how the theatres can reposition themselves to profit most from new markets

- Positioning a snack manufacturer to enter China, determining types of snacks most wanted, and assessing the market's willingness to pay for snacks

- Determining the value of a PC manufacturer on a stand-alone basis and suggesting possible acquirers to help divest itself of non-core businesses

Leading European strategy consulting firms include:

- Boston Consulting Group
- McKinsey & Company
- Roland Berger
- Bain & Company

In addition, there are several strong local Tier 2 consultancies. In the UK, OC&C, Commercial Advantage and Corven are successful examples in this category.

Visit **Vault Europe's Consulting Career Channel** at **www.Vault.com/Europe** for insider firm profiles, employee surveys of consultants in Europe, job listings, expert consulting career advice, insider salary information and more.

VAULT CAREER LIBRARY 27

Operations Consulting

Operations consultants examine a client's internal workings, such as production processes, distribution, order fulfilment, and customer service. While strategy consultants set the firm's goals, operations consultants ensure that clients reach these goals. Operations consultants investigate customer service response times, cut operating or inventory backlog costs, or look into resource allocation. They improve distribution, heighten product quality, or restructure departments and organisations (a specialty of the "re-engineering" craze of the early 1990s).

Unlike strategic consultants, who tend to hand off their findings and leave, operations consultants generally assist in assuring implementation of their suggestions. Major consulting firms now offer both strategic and operations services.

Examples of typical operations consulting engagements:

• Streamlining the equipment purchasing process of a major tyre manufacturer

• Determining how a restaurant chain can save on ingredient costs without changing its menu

• Working with a newly-merged commercial bank to increase its customer response efficiency

• Creating a new logistical database for a tyre manufacturer

Leading operations consulting firms include:

• Accenture

• Capgemini

• Deloitte

• IBM Consulting

Information Technology Consulting

Information Technology (or "IT") consultants help clients achieve their business goals. IT consultants (also called systems consultants) work with corporations and other clients to understand how they can best leverage technology for the organisation. They design custom software or networking solutions, test for system and program the compatibility, and ensure that the new system is properly implemented.

Most IT consultants, by definition, boast sharply honed technical skills. But IT solutions must be implemented as an overall part of a business solution. Otherwise, clients are sure to scream for cost-justification and/or fire their IT department heads for wasting money when solutions start to fail.

Examples of typical IT consulting engagements:

- Testing an investment bank's vulnerability to hackers
- Converting a commercial bank's mainframe system into an Oracle-based client-server environment
- Implementing a firewall for a retail chain's customer service servers
- Upgrading a major law firm from a word processing application to an operating system
- Troubleshooting on a major SAP software installation (software used by companies to manage accounting, personnel, inventory and other issues)

Leading information technology firms include:

- Accenture
- Computer Sciences Corporation (CSC)
- Electronic Data Systems (EDS)

Visit **Vault Europe's Consulting Career Channel** at **www.Vault.com/Europe** for insider firm profiles, employee surveys of consultants in Europe, job listings, expert consulting career advice, insider salary information and more.

VAULT CAREER LIBRARY 29

Human Resources Consulting

The best business strategies, the most up-to-date technologies, and most streamlined operations mean nothing if no one can put them into place. That's why HR consulting is on the upswing. Increasingly, companies have concluded that investing in their human capital pays off. Human resources consultants maximise the value of employees while placing the right people with the right skills in the right roles. This kind of HR consulting, also known as organisational development or change management, has been one of the hottest consulting fields in recent years. Studies and advice around creating diversity and work/life balance have been popular topics.

However, industry experts are doubtful whether the market for this type of HR consulting will continue to grow. HR consulting is often considered a long-term luxury. As companies are required to respond more and more in the short-term to stock market demands, HR consulting has to respond more to practical demands such as organisational restructuring or systems implementations.

HR consultants also provide technical advice. This advice is largely based on number crunching, and those who excel at it are generally known as actuaries. Actuarial advice focuses on restructuring benefits packages and valuating compensation structures, among other technical assignments. Actuarial consultants must pass many certification exams throughout their careers to remain eligible to practice their trade.

Examples of typical human resources consulting engagements:

- Bringing together the cultures of merged companies by developing or altering work cultures
- "Managing relationships" to ensure focus on customers and open communication
- Building "competencies" through better and more efficient training programmes
- Fostering employee creativity through "process innovation"
- Counselling and processing redundant employees and assisting them in finding new jobs
- Creating or updating a new division's benefits package
- Reviewing and revising a law firm's compensation structure

Leading human resources consulting firms include:

- Hewitt Associates
- Towers Perrin
- Watson Wyatt Worldwide
- Mercer Human Resource Consulting

Boutique Consulting Firms

Boutique firms support their clients with highly-specialised expertise. Boutique firms choose to focus on a smaller number of industries (energy, life sciences, retail), functions (M&A, economics and litigation, turnaround), or methodologies (real options, EVA).

There are a couple of common misconceptions about boutique firms. One is that being a "boutique consulting firm" necessarily implies being a small firm. This is not the case. A boutique is determined not by size, but by focus. L.E.K. Consulting (which was founded by a handful of former Bain partners) has roughly 500 employees, but we would consider the company a boutique because of its specific focus on three types of strategy consulting problems-M&A, shareholder value, and business strategy. Another misconception is that boutiques are less prestigious than the multi-functional firms. This highly depends on the area of focus. For example, BCG is extremely well-regarded across many industries for most types of strategy problems, but for a decision analysis or real options strategy problem, clients might turn to Strategic Decisions Group, which focuses on those areas.

All this said, we should note that many boutiques are indeed small, ranging from somewhere under 200 employees to a single consultant. Often, boutique consulting firms grow from the expertise and client relationships of one to five founding partners, and unless it sells a consistently large flow of work, the firm has no compelling reason to grow quickly. Also, smaller boutiques can deliver services at lower costs than the larger consultancies because a smaller firm requires less overhead and less extra "capacity" (i.e. consultants), so their services might seem more attractive to prospective clients than those of the more expensive firms.

If you are especially interested in a particular industry or type of consulting problem, definitely do your homework on the outstanding boutiques in that field. If you find the right company to match your interests, you will spend all of your time doing the work you dreamt of, and that is a much harder goal to achieve within a more diverse consulting firm.

Visit **Vault Europe's Consulting Career Channel** at **www.Vault.com/Europe** for insider firm profiles, employee surveys of consultants in Europe, job listings, expert consulting career advice, insider salary information and more.

VAULT CAREER LIBRARY

31

Examples of boutique consulting projects:

- A consulting firm with a well-known shareholder value methodology helps a beverage company establish value metrics in its business units

- An economics consulting firm helps a foreign government decide how to structure the privatisation (sale) of its utilities through an auction

- A niche R&D strategy consulting firm deploys two consultants to a high-growth semiconductor company in Silicon Valley for a 3 month project to improve R&D processes

- A process reengineering boutique snares a 6-month project to assist implementation of new supplier standards for an automotive consortium

- A turnaround consulting firm helps a telecommunications hardware firm restructure its organisation to avoid insolvency

Leading boutique and internal consulting firms include:

- L.E.K. Consulting (shareholder value, M&A, and business strategy)

- Marakon Associates (shareholder value methodology)

- OC & C (consumer goods & retail)

- IGD (a grocery retail specialist)

In addition, there are numerous specialist consultancies that provide expert advice for specific industry segments. Examples are PMSI, who have built a strong reputation in the drinks industry or First Marine, who are experts in shipbuilding and shipyards.

Internal Consulting Firms

Recognising a constant need for third-party expertise, some corporations have established internal consulting units. Consultants from these units report to a central consulting division, who then staffs its employees within different business units in the company for assistance on issues such as corporate strategy, business development, and project management. The consultants remain deployed with the client for either a set period of time or throughout the duration of a specific project. Even though everyone technically works for the same company, the consulting arm acts as an outsider, since its consultants don't work for the business units.

Why don't these corporations keep hiring outside consultancies? One reason corporations like having internal consulting groups is cost savings. Internal consulting groups can be an economical way to obtain a large amount of consulting help. The firm doesn't have to pay the exorbitant billing rates; instead, it can receive the outsider opinion for a corporate pay scale. The firm also benefits from having a dedicated team of experts knowledgeable on the company and its industry. In addition, having a dedicated internal consulting unit is a smart way for corporations to market themselves and attract top talent from the outside consulting ranks.

You should think of internal consulting as the same role as if you were in a typical external consulting firm, except on permanent retainer for the same client. You are simply on the client side of the table, and your salary comes directly from the client. The main disadvantages of being an internal consultant instead of a "normal" consultant is that you don't get the same variety of industries as you would elsewhere, and you are paid at corporate salaries, which are typically lower than consultant salaries. On the other hand, you will no doubt travel less. And because you are not trying to win repeat work as a consultancy, you will not have the same face time pressures that you might as a typical management consultant.

So, if you are especially concerned about issues like travel and hours, but you are attracted to the types of problems consultants face, you might find an internal consulting arm to be a great fit for you. Note that such departments are not always called "internal consulting" (they are sometimes called "corporate strategy" or "strategic planning"), so you'll have to do some digging. Also, you should bear in mind that positions within these departments are few and hard to come by, particularly if you have no previous consulting experience. Companies will normally either recruit gifted individuals from their own ranks or attempt to attract seasoned consultants, in order to acquire not only an experienced professional but also the skill set that comes with him.

Examples of internal consulting projects:

- The internal consulting arm of a large commodity trading business deploys three consultants to help its futures brokerage arm with a marketing strategy.

- An internal consulting group at a large petrochemicals corporation hires a change management specialist for long-term deployment on a project with the marketing distribution operating unit, to assist in a multi-year implementation of SAP system

Visit **Vault Europe's Consulting Career Channel** at **www.Vault.com/Europe** for insider firm profiles, employee surveys of consultants in Europe, job listings, expert consulting career advice, insider salary information and more.

VAULT CAREER LIBRARY 33

Representative internal consulting practices include:

- American Express Strategic Planning Group
- JPMorgan Internal Consulting Services
- Johnson & Johnson Decision Sciences Group

To get the inside scoop on top consulting employers, read:

The Vault Guide to the Top 25 Consulting Firms, European Edition – This best-selling guide features insider profiles of the top consulting firms in Europe. Based on surveys and interviews of thousands of consulting professionals, this guide also includes Vault's exclusive Top 50 Consulting Firms prestige rankings.

Vault Consulting Employer Profiles – For detailed 50-page insider reports on individual firms, get Vault's employer profiles. Profiles include McKinsey, Bain, Boston Consulting Group, Booz Allen, Accenture and many more.

Go to the Vault Europe Consulting Career Channel at www.Vault.com/Europe

CAREER
GUIDE

GETTING
HIRED

CONSULTING

Targeting Consulting Firms

CHAPTER 3

By now you've decided to pursue a career in consulting. You've spoken to real-life consultants, had a heart-to-heart with your career advisor, and made peace with the potential for long hours and brutal travel in exchange for intriguing project work and financial rewards. Now it's time to get started and choose where you'd like to work.

Researching Companies, the Right Way

Landing a consulting job takes a lot of time and effort, and company research plays an important role in a candidate's preparation. Prior to the 1990s, information on companies was not very easy to find. Candidates relied on word-of-mouth insights, company literature, or the occasional book. With the advent of the Internet, the process of researching a company changed dramatically. Candidates are now expected to read a company's web site, understand the company's makeup and be prepared to talk about it in interviews. Avoiding this step in your preparation can be the difference between a job offer and a rejection letter.

Company basics

With all the information on potential employers readily available, it's all too easy to overdose. Consulting firms do not expect you to be an expert; they merely want you to have a basic grasp of their firm's history, current practice areas and targeted industries, major office locations, recent news developments and what key factors distinguish them from their competition. The important thing is to show genuine interest in the consulting industry as a whole, the problem-solving prowess to excel as a consultant, and the personal skills to work well with both the client and your project team.

Be comfortable with the basics of each firm, but don't let your research become an end in itself. Overzealous candidates often make this mistake. They feel compelled to ask three-layered questions about revenue streams and utilisation rates to show recruiters just how much they prepared for the first interview. Recruiters are not particularly impressed by this behaviour. On the other hand, they have even less patience for candidates who exhibit no knowledge of the firm whatsoever.

Visit **Vault Europe's Consulting Career Channel** at **www.Vault.com/Europe** for insider firm profiles, employee surveys of consultants in Europe, job listings, expert consulting career advice, insider salary information and more.

VAULT CAREER LIBRARY 37

Core competencies

Keep your research simple and focused. Go to a firm's web site and learn the basics, making sure to find out the firm's core competencies or the skill sets that it expects each new hire to have. You should read the firm's annual report if it is publicly traded. If you are still in university, look up the firm of your dreams on Lexis/Nexis and look for recent articles on the firm.

A firm's core competencies can have a big impact on its culture, so knowing them will help you decide if the work environment will be agreeable. Remember, company research is not just to help you do well in an interview; it also will help you decide if the firm is where you want to be.

How do they interview?

Aside from learning about a company through its web site, you could benefit from knowing how the firm interviews. Do they ask case questions? Are there multiple interview rounds? Does the firm use interview panels, or is each interview conducted in a one-on-one format? Getting this information before the interview can lower your stress level and make you a more relaxed candidate. The best source is people you may know at the firm or friends who have gone through the interview process already. You can even address these questions to company recruiters. Armed with this information, your focus on the day of the interview will be much sharper, and your discussions will cover only the topics that matter most. (For insider information on the hiring process at top consulting firms, see the Vault Guide to the Top 50 Consulting Firms and Vault's consulting firm Employer Profiles.)

A little goes a long way

Once you've done all the necessary research on a firm, store it away in your memory for the actual interview. Use it in a very limited fashion, or mix it into discussions about your work experience, your personality, and your goals. Think of your newfound company knowledge as a fail-safe cushion for questions such as "Why do you want to work here?" and "What is it about our firm that interests you?" A little company information goes a long way with these questions. Leave your doctoral thesis at home, and do not be afraid to express your ignorance on certain topics. Recruiters appreciate a certain level of intellectual humility.

Understanding the Different Firms

Your mission: find a firm that fits with your current goals and lifestyle and provides you with the experience you need for your next career move.

The truth is, very few of us will be lucky enough to have multiple job offers and have to make a job decision based on such specific criteria as the firm's travel model. Use the information you gather to eliminate firms you definitely wouldn't work at. But we encourage you to not be overly picky in your search. Keep an open mind — a firm you aren't in love with might wind up your only job offer.

Here is a short list of questions to help you understand the firms a little better. You might ask the following questions at the time of an interview or during your research phase.

What kind of consulting projects does the firm typically encounter?

Are you interested in working on high-level strategy issues, or do you prefer to roll your sleeves up and dig into the operational details of a company? How important is it for you to be involved in the actual implementation of the strategy? Would you prefer to spend all of your time in one industry? See how employers fit with your preferences. Understanding yourself and your potential employers yields vital information about firms' working style and culture — and your suitability there.

Do analysts/associates work on more than one project (also known as an engagement or study) simultaneously?

Some companies, like McKinsey and Booz Allen Hamilton, assign their associates and analysts to a single project at any given time. Others, like BCG, prefer to staff consultants on up to five engagements at once. This results in a number of differences in working style.

• When on a number of studies at once, you cannot get everything done in the time available. Therefore, you must become adept at managing expectations and delineating complex priorities and trade-offs.

• If you plan on consulting for just a couple of years, consider your goals for breadth and depth of exposure to industries and study types. Judge if you prefer to dig into fewer areas in greater detail or to get maximum exposure to a wide range of experiences.

Visit **Vault Europe's Consulting Career Channel** at www.Vault.com/Europe for insider firm profiles, employee surveys of consultants in Europe, job listings, expert consulting career advice, insider salary information and more.

VAULT CAREER LIBRARY 39

- Working on multiple projects normally means that you spend more time in the office than at the client's — after all, sitting at Client A's office discussing Client B's distribution problems on the telephone would be unprofessional. Be aware, however, that two or more clients means more opportunities for emergencies and hastily-called meetings that require your presence.

- Single projects generally last from a few weeks up to a year (or longer on some occasions). By the end of the project, depending on staffing needs, you might find yourself unwillingly pigeonholed into an area of expertise.

Do project teams include both consultants and full-time client members?

While almost all consulting firms mention "considerable client contact" as one of their attributes, examine this further. Discern if this means weekly meetings with senior client managers or daily interaction with client staff who provide full-time support to the project. Again, the answer to your query indicates a lot about the style of your projected work patterns:

- On the one hand, client team members can be burdensome. They expect you to spend time schooling them in your consulting methodologies and pulling them through the "wallow phase" (when there's just too much information). They also need you to adjust your schedule to their other commitments.

- On the other hand, working with client team members can be the most valuable way for a consultant to spend his or her time. For one thing, you start to develop management skills (something many consultants lack). You also gain better insight into your client's industry and company (which is especially valuable if you ever want to consider jumping ship to a client at some point).

What is the travel model?

Some consultants enjoy extensive travel (and the accompanying frequent flyer miles) while others loathe the prospect of getting stuck at yet another airport lounge. Whichever type you are, learn about the firm's travel model. Firms like Accenture, Booz Allen Hamilton, and McKinsey typically keep their consultants on client site four days a week, with Fridays in the office. Bain and BCG, on average, spend a lot of time at client sites at the beginning and end of the project, but somewhat less in between. While every project has different travel needs, firms do have standard travel policies.

Also find out what proportion of engagements tend to be out of town. Nearly all of the large consulting firms work from offices in most major locations around the world. More localised competitors like Monitor usually send their consultants to faraway destinations for extended periods because they normally don't have a physical presence near the client.

Does the consulting firm have offices worldwide, or is it based in a small number of key cities? How does this compare with its client distribution?

Ask about the firm's policy on staffing between offices. Some consultancies take a more pan-regional approach to staffing projects, especially in European and Asian offices. This means that even if you work in the London office, you might find yourself shipped off to Hungary or Chiang Mai. Consulting firms with strong specialisations are also more prone to send consultants on extended trips — specialised assignments require the best consultants, no matter where they might be based.

Also ask about how each firm distributes its offices: geographically or by specialty. While most firms today organise their offices geographically, some still retain what are commonly called "Centres of Excellence" (or COEs). If you work for a COE, you will probably report geographically to that office, meaning you will most likely maintain your residence nearby. Some firms, like DiamondCluster International, allow consultants to live anywhere and work out of any of their offices, though they still must report administratively to the COE. Keep in mind that where you live impacts how far you travel and how long you stay away from home.

At what level do consultants begin to specialise by industry, function, or geographic expertise?

As you enter consulting, you might have a clear idea of an industry or functional area in which you wish to specialise. On the other hand, you might want to use consulting to remain industry-neutral in the short term, while assessing your options. Almost every firm encourages its consultants to choose an area of expertise as they increase in tenure; the question is, how quickly?

Most big strategy firms prefer their new recruits follow a generalist track for a few years before specialising. That said, once you complete a few successful projects in a particular area, you are often asked to do others in that area. At other firms, you are hired specifically for your current skill base. All firms encourage training (at least in theory), but training generally relates specifically to your current skills. All this amounts to what is commonly called "pigeonholing," or getting stuck in a specialisation.

Visit **Vault Europe's Consulting Career Channel** at **www.Vault.com/Europe** for insider firm profiles, employee surveys of consultants in Europe, job listings, expert consulting career advice, insider salary information and more.

V∧ULT   C A R E E R
L I B R A R Y   **41**

What else?

To complete your picture of the firm, you may want to find out a few other details. These include (but aren't limited to): turnover rate, holiday policy, unpaid leave policy, telecommuting options, feedback system, and social atmosphere. Again, think about what is particularly important to you, and ask away. You may want to wait until you receive an offer to get into every last detail, however; otherwise, you'll look as if you're only concerned with the leave policy or free drinks.

To get the inside scoop on top consulting employers, read:

The Vault Guide to the Top 25 Consulting Firms, European Edition – This best-selling guide features insider profiles of the top consulting firms in Europe. Based on surveys and interviews of thousands of consulting professionals, this guide also includes Vault's exclusive Top 50 Consulting Firms prestige rankings.

Vault Consulting Employer Profiles – For detailed 50-page insider reports on individual firms, get Vault's employer profiles. Profiles include McKinsey, Bain, Boston Consulting Group, Booz Allen, Accenture and many more.

Go to the Vault Europe Consulting Career Channel at www.Vault.com/Europe

Interviewing the Consultants

Talking to current consultants at the firm of your choice is the best way to get the background you want.

Think about the way you ask questions. For example, people are bad answering questions like "What's a typical day?" or "What are the projects like?" Their answers might be vague, or perhaps they might tell you about the best three projects they worked on out of twenty, which is not the answer you're looking for. Instead of asking for a typical day, ask how he or she spent yesterday. Instead of asking to describe a few projects, ask for the last three. Instead of asking how many hours he or she typically works, ask how many hours he or she worked over the past two weeks.

You can take things a step further, however, and ask scenario questions. These can be fun to ask and can give you more truthful answers, especially when it comes to lifestyle-related questions. Here are some examples. If you're nervy enough, you can even ask your interviewer one or two of these!

• If you have a spare evening from work, how would you spend it?
• With your work schedule, could you commit to a Monday evening class at 6 p.m. at the local university? Or Thursday tickets to a concert season?
• When did you come into work yesterday? When did you leave?
• When you and your colleagues go out for dinner or drinks, where do you go?
• How many Sundays did you work this year?
• How many times will you check your voice mail tonight?
• What business applications, such as Word, Excel, or @RISK, have you used for your reports? Your client presentations? Your financial models?
• Have you ever had to cancel dinner with your spouse at the last minute because of work?
• If you were managing partner of your firm, what would you change about it?

You get the idea. Think about what's really important to you, and find a vivid way to ask it.

Most people are able to find current consultants to speak with at their target firms. We offer the following idea: talk to former employees of the firm. They will have different (and occasionally more candid) opinions on the firm than will current employees.

There are two categories of former employees you should consider talking with:

• *Former employees who are still in consulting.* Why did the consultant leave? What did he like about the firm? What did he dislike? What does he find more appealing about his current firm? Would he work for the firm again, given the opportunity?

Visit **Vault Europe's Consulting Career Channel** at **www.Vault.com/Europe** for insider firm profiles, employee surveys of consultants in Europe, job listings, expert consulting career advice, insider salary information and more.

VAULT CAREER LIBRARY **43**

- *Former employees who are no longer in consulting.* Why did the person leave the consulting industry altogether? Was it this specific firm that turned him off to the industry as a whole, or was it simply the industry? What does he find about his current career more compelling than a consulting career, and what does he like better about the firm versus his current place of employment?

The Hiring Process

CHAPTER 4

The Recruiting Process: An Overview

The most valuable asset of any consulting firm is its human capital. Before clients see presentations, reports, or results, they see consultants. Before clients work with products or services, they work with people. Consequently, consulting firms purposefully make their interviews intense and lengthy to measure your intellectual, physical and emotional stamina.

For a long time, consulting firms focused on recruiting a relatively small number of undergraduate and graduate institutions. When the dot-com boom occurred in the late 1990s, Internet start-ups that offered leadership positions and the smell of an early retirement stole many highly-qualified students away from the consulting firms. Realising they might be missing out on talent elsewhere, consulting firms began to take a more open-minded approach to recruiting, including considering candidates with non-traditional advanced degrees, such as MDs or PhDs.

Recruitment channels

On-campus milkrounds is still the predominant recruitment channel for most consultancies. However, with increasing competition, high employee turnover rates and the need for offering tailored solutions for clients, consultancies are now considering a wider range of backgrounds and application methods. Your best recruitment channel may simply depend on the time of the year. Bear in mind that most graduates join companies in the autumn. However, bonuses are normally paid in December, so relatively few consultants would resign at this time of the year. So, if you are applying outside the milkrounds you might snap up a good offer in the early parts of the year when consultancies are looking to fill their resourcing gaps quickly.

These are the three main recruitment processes that consultancies follow. All three have variants:

• Milkrounds are the most common recruiting channels at undergraduate or MBA schools, but there are also recruitment fairs, competitions and social events which consultancies use to preselect candidates.

Visit **Vault Europe's Consulting Career Channel** at **www.Vault.com/Europe** for insider firm profiles, employee surveys of consultants in Europe, job listings, expert consulting career advice, insider salary information and more.

VAULT CAREER LIBRARY 45

- Direct applications can be via email, post or online application forms and include responding to newspaper ads, getting recommended by someone in the organisation who knows you or just having an unsolicited shot at it.

- Recruitment agencies come in various formats. There are ample differences between them, mainly depending on the depth of search and selection that they go into. Senior-level headhunters who work for months on only one placement are one end of the spectrum, while others simply pool and distribute CVs.

Your best channel for getting hired by a consultancy depends on the following factors:

    1. Your level and capabilities

    2. The size and type of your target company

    3. The time of the year.

Even if you've just finished your MBA top of the class, have five years of industry and consulting experience, and on the side created a couple of successful business ventures, you might want to consider the different recruitment channel options as they also offer differences in entry level and pay.

Milkrounds and recruitment fairs

The exact process varies by school, firm and country. In most cases, company representatives will present the firm at an event and will be available to answer your questions in a wider forum. They may accept your CV and in some cases even interview you at the event, but bear in mind that you should use the information gathered at the event to tailor your application to the company's needs. Normally, applications will be considered for a few weeks after the event. If your background matches the target profile, you will be invited to a first round of interviews, quite often at the campus. If you pass, there will normally be at least one more round of interviews at the company's office, giving you a chance to get a feel for the environment in which you will spend most of your days, evenings (and potentially nights) for the next few years.

A few years ago, assessment centres used to be a popular selection method for graduates. At assessment centres, a number of candidates are invited at the same time and asked to complete a number of job-related tasks, some individually, some in a group. The aim is to test not only your intellectual skills, but also your team behaviour and stress handling capabilities. This may look like a good idea for selecting consultants, as you will be working in teams on most consulting projects. However, most consultancies have given up on assessment centres. On the one hand, they are costly and difficult to set up properly. On the other hand, they are a poor reflection of the true work environment and have often failed to provide the right candidates. It can be hard to be a good team player while competing with your "team mates" for a job.

Direct applications

Business schools and some of the more practical European universities have adopted the British model of campus universities and defined schedules leading up to graduation. However, many of the more academic universities across Europe allow graduates to complete their studies in their own time. As a result, milkrounds are a less common feature on the continent, and consultancies are likely to consider candidates throughout the year. You will be able to judge current demand through their websites and newspaper adverts and be invited to apply directly, either through an application form or with a traditional application letter. The right timing is key for direct applications, so make sure you speak to someone who knows the company well to master the supply and demand cycles.

The disadvantage of direct applications is that you'll be competing for the recruiter's attention against hundreds of mail-merged applications from around the world of which very few will actually match the job spec. If at all possible, try to establish a contact with the recruiter or — even better — a current consultant at the company who can make sure that your application is being considered.

Recruitment agencies

Recruitment agencies are attractive to both employers and job seekers, as they take over parts of the search and selection process on both sides. In theory, this "matchmaking" capability should enhance the chances of finding good job-candidate matches. In reality, many recruitment agencies operate a simple mail in — mail out model where CVs are simply forwarded to numerous companies.

In dealing with recruitment agencies, it's essential that you understand their rules before sending them your CV. Think of the following analogy: If you were to buy a house, would you consider the one that has been advertised for months and months by all the real estate agents in town? Or do you want to snap up the needle-in-the-haystack property as soon as it appears on the books of an agent you trust? If you go through a recruitment agent, make sure that you know exactly who they are sending your CV to and how close their relationship with the target company is.

Recruitment agents can help you in many ways; in finding the right company for your profile, in preparing your CV, in determining the right timing for your application, in

Visit **Vault Europe's Consulting Career Channel** at **www.Vault.com/Europe** for insider firm profiles, employee surveys of consultants in Europe, job listings, expert consulting career advice, insider salary information and more.

VAULT CAREER LIBRARY   47

finding out the truth behind a rejection, and finally in negotiating salaries. However, be aware that only the reputable ones will think of you as a potential "repeat customer" and hence think of your interests as much as they think of their own.

Well known recruitment agencies in the UK consulting market are:

- Woodhurst
- BLT
- BYT
- Michael Page
- Prism

How to get selected

It will always be easier to get hired as an MBA or recent graduate, however, here are ways you can increase your chances of being selected for an interview.

Keep in mind that there are many steps to take in order to get to the interview process. It is competitive just to get an on-campus interview; when firms choose not to come to your campus, or if you are trying to break in from another industry without contacts, the competition is much stiffer. Here's how to get those precious interviews.

For each firm in which you are interested, you will want to

1. Tailor your CV and experiences for consulting.
2. Find the appropriate contact, either through on-campus recruiting or networking. (You can ask an alumnus to point you to the right contact, for example.)
3. Apply to the firm by crafting a covering letter specific to the firm, delivering it to the firm, and following up by e-mail or phone.
4. Arrive at the interview prepared and appropriately dressed.

Tailoring Your CV for Consulting

Consulting firms receive thousands of applications each year, both during recruiting season and otherwise. Your CV serves as an important tool for recruiters in the selection/elimination process. You increase your selection chances by tailoring your CV and covering letter to specific consulting firms and positions. Consulting recruiters look for the following on CVs:

- **Evidence of academic strength.** Some firms insist on this information and even set UCAS point requirements. Scores are usually more important for undergraduates than MBAs or career changers.

- **Team player characteristics.** Consulting firms structure their teams very carefully. Some of them use complicated matrices to determine the best fit for each project based on available resources, necessary skills, and training plans. Recruiters want people who can play their roles with flexibility and grace.

- **Propensity for leadership and confidence.** Consulting firms want employees with a senior management potential. They see all recruits as either future partners or future clients. Consulting firms want to work with employees who already demonstrate a predisposition to leadership, not someone who needs to be taught from scratch. Evidence of such potential includes leadership positions held in university and/or the undertaking of new initiatives without support.

- **Accomplishments.** Firms seek people who boast long lists of accomplishments that demonstrate reliability, tenacity, commitment, motivation, and high standards of excellence. Clients want to hire consultants who can get things done well, in a short amount of time and without too much hassle.

- **Distinctions.** You've got lots of competition. However, if you can differentiate yourself on your CV — highlighting technical skills, foreign languages, publications, awards, notable public appearances — it will be to your advantage.

In some cases, recruiters look for relevant functional expertise (e.g. engineering or finance) or for specific industry experience or technical skills. If you know this ahead of time, emphasise any germane experiences you have. Wherever possible, quantify your results to make your achievements more concrete and tangible.

Be aware that how you write and structure your CV says a lot about how you communicate with others. Make your CV as terse as possible, and make your layout easy on the eyes. A consultant's time is worth many hundreds of pounds per hour, and your client's time is

Visit **Vault Europe's Consulting Career Channel** at **www.Vault.com/Europe** for insider firm profiles, employee surveys of consultants in Europe, job listings, expert consulting career advice, insider salary information and more.

VAULT CAREER LIBRARY 49

equally important. No one involved has enough patience to read through copious paragraphs, so learn to use bullet points and get to the bottom line.

What are the Most Sought After Traits?

While you can sign up to study accounting, corporate finance or management at many a university, you will not find a course under the name of consulting. That is because consulting doesn't comprise one defined set of skills; consultants are often specialists at being generalists. Here are 4 areas that are considered of importance by future employers

Broad interests

A healthy dose of interest in a broad range of subjects is paramount for a successful career. The subjects that you will deal with during your consulting career are likely to be varied, often shifting beween industries as far apart as high-fashion clothing and waste management. If you can pick up a copy of The Economist and find an interesting side to many of the articles, that is a good start.

Analysis

As a consultant, one of your core competencies is your ability to analyse complex subject matters in an effective and sensible way, and any successful consultant will have a an above-average ability of analysis. Are you generally known to be able to grasp the abstract and simplify problems? Do your friends consider you a person of reason? If you answered the questions positively then chances are you have 'consulted' already.

Internationality

With projects often spanning larger regions or even the world, consultants are required to feel at ease with international exposure, be it travel, foreign clients or information sources. This is especially true in European consulting markets, and has led firms to consider 'internationality' as an increasingly relevant criterion of hire. Consultants speaking multiple languages and with experiences in multiple countries (studies, travel or other) can be staffed on a wider variety of projects and locations, making them more valuable for the firm.

Communication

The work of a consultant is useless unless it can be communicated in the right way, and therefore excellent communication skills are key. You will be required to express yourself in an engaging and precise manner in both written and spoken form, and mastering this is one of the keys to a successful career.

How to Strengthen a Non-Business CV

It is true that consulting firms love to hire candidates with direct experience in business. Many don't have it. The good news is that you can strengthen your CV significantly by reframing your experiences in consultant language.

Keep in mind how consultants think: they assess the situation, define the problem, identify the solution and execute. They also look for management potential, leadership qualities and soft skills. You wouldn't be interested in consulting if you hadn't had similar experiences in your life, would you? For example, how did you research and identify your history thesis topic? You had to invent a methodology and answer an interesting question. Are you a doctor? Then every day you use situation assessments and hypotheses. Did you tutor a student part-time in calculus? Then you will likely be a solid people manager.

The following is an excerpt from a CV of an MBA student. Prior to business school, he worked for a fictitious investment bank called Smart Brothers as a computer programmer. He is knowledgeable in C++ and Oracle and spent 80 hours a week in front of a monitor coding financial software engines and Windows applications. His challenge was to reflect skills that would interest a consulting firm. Here is how he wrote up his work experience:

Visit **Vault Europe's Consulting Career Channel** at **www.Vault.com/Europe** for insider firm profiles, employee surveys of consultants in Europe, job listings, expert consulting career advice, insider salary information and more.

VAULT CAREER LIBRARY 51

SMART BROTHERS London, United Kingdom

Project Manager – Information Technology   June 2001 – July 2006

- Managed project teams to develop profit and loss systems for Proprietary Trading group

- Promoted to project leadership role in two years, well ahead of department average of four

- Developed an original mathematical algorithm for trading processing module, improving performance by 1200%

- Led team of six analysts in firmwide project to re-engineer loan syndicate trading flows in firm's largest technology project of 1999. Recommendations established new firmwide standard for real-time trade processing

- Appointed lead developer of interest accrual team after just three months in department. Initiated and designed project to create customised, improved interest accrual and P&L applications for fixed income controllers

- Selected to work on high-profile project to re-engineer corporate bond trading P&L system. Reduced overnight processing time from six hours to 20 minutes and improved desktop application speed by 350%

- Devoted 20-25 hours a month instructing junior members of the team on interest accrual and trading

---

Note that this person doesn't speak to the content of his work as much as the process. We have no idea what kinds of software he really built or what computer languages he knows. On the other hand, we know that he managed teams, was dedicated enough to his job to achieve a fast promotion, and was committed to building the knowledge base of his team. He also worked closely with his client base of users in order to solve their problems. In addition, he wrote a very results-focused set of bullet points, for example quantifying the performance improvements or mentioning how he established a new standard. This CV suggests not programmer, but consultant.

The moral of the story is to think carefully about your past experiences and reframe them as if they were consulting projects; you will be pleasantly surprised and recruiters will be impressed.

Sample Covering Letters and CVs

Elizabeth Jenkins
Director of Postgraduate Recruitment
Bath Analytics
Clarendon House
Conduit Street
London
W1X 5HX

2 November, 2006

Dear Elizabeth,

I am writing to introduce myself as a candidate for a consulting position at your firm. As you may know I contacted one of your consultants, Angela Schindler, last summer regarding her article on "Assessing Risks in the Packaged Food Industry" in your quarterly magazine. I read this article as part of my postgraduate studies in Economics at the London School of Economics and was interested in her views on resulting management implications. The depth and thoroughness of her article and our discussion reinforced my belief that Bath Analytics is a highly professional consulting firm tackling real and fascinating strategic problems on a daily basis.

I honed my problem solving skills as a Category Manager with Unilever where I was directly responsible for, and spent much of my time interacting with, both internal and external customers. As a key touch-point for sales, marketing, finance, accounting and operations I managed multiple costing, launch, co-marketing and retail projects to a 3% sales increase in a shrinking market and business unit.

My ability to excel in a variety of professional and personal spheres has been further demonstrated during this past year as I led a team selected 1st of 25 competitors to represent the LSE at an international business competition, while training and playing as a varsity athlete, helping coordinate a world-class forum on Peruvian economic development, organising/participating in a charity hitch-hike to Lourdes and acting as President of the University of London Sports and Social Committee.

I feel my ability to synthesise data, structure complex problems, and communicate effectively with people from a variety of backgrounds would help Bath Analytics add value in the professional sphere and build lasting, effective relationships with its clients.

I hope to hear from your firm shortly, and will follow up with you next week.

Yours sincerely,
Mark Patzing

Visit **Vault Europe's Consulting Career Channel** at www.Vault.com/Europe for insider firm profiles, employee surveys of consultants in Europe, job listings, expert consulting career advice, insider salary information and more.

VAULT CAREER LIBRARY   53

MARK PATZING

mark.patzing@lse.ac.uk   +44(0)795 765 5546

EDUCATION

2005-2007	London School of Economics
	Completing Masters in Economics
1997-2001	Will Green University (Melbourne, Australia)
	Bachelor Degree — Physics

WORK EXPERIENCE

2003-05 Unilever   **Sydney, Australia**
Category Manager

• Wide range of direct and varied client exposure through three promotions in two years
• Nominated 'Unilever Sales Awards of Excellence' 2004, recognising the top 5% of sales organisation
• Led team to sales increase of 6% ($1.2 million) by initiating. structuring and coordinating programs to support direct sales force of 50+ executing chain-wide promotions
• Negotiated volume, pricing, shelf, and merchandising activity by distilling and leveraging complex consumption analytics and market data to tailor spending, media, and strategy programs to customers' consumers
• Managed logistics, customer expectations and retail space in implementing 'opencode dating' program across Sydney: resulting inventory loss <1% ($70,000), sales increase 8%
• Frequently selected to advise senior management on credit, operational and procedural initiatives resulting in improved accounts receivable lag times from roughly 180 to 30 days

2002-03 Garder Consulting   **Melbourne, Australia**
Researcher/Analyst

• Initiated independent study of high potential industry sectors, resulting in firm strategy shift from marketing and customer support (initial business drivers) to risk and cost reduction
• Conducted market research for, and about potential clients by compiling and analysing banking industry businesses resulting in sale of major consulting assignment and on-going business

2001-02 International Language Institute   **Taipei, Taiwan**
English Instructor

• Developed and implemented curriculum at high school/ university levels by integrating fragmented materials; increasing student retention by 20% and class size by 50%
• Selected to design and deliver interactive program to executives aimed at facilitating group discussion and knowledge growth; led to contract extension and increased business referrals

1996-00 (Summers) Camp Narnin   **Narnin, Australia**
Director

• Managed, trained, motivated, coordinated and supervised staff of 100+; resulting in record setting camper enrolment (20% increase) and higher staff retention rate of roughly 65%
• Conducted leadership and management seminars utilising team dynamic/group building techniques to build trust and interpersonal skills, increasing promotion rate among participants

ADDITIONAL INFORMATION

Volunteer:	President, University of London Sports & Social Committee,
	Will Green Buddies: screened, supervised & motivated 70+ student volunteers
Achievements:	Selected to represent London School of Economics at International Business Competition (1st of 45 projects)
Interests:	Sport — LSU Varsity Athlete (Squash — 1st VII), Yacht racing. World travel
Languages:	French (Conversant), Mandarin (Basic)

MICHEL DACOURT

mob +44 (0) 7993 815926 - mdacourt@gmail.com

Date and place of birth: May 12th, 1979 in Madrid, Spain   *Nationality:* French

WORK EXPERIENCE

2005-07   **Siemens Business Services**   London, UK

IT Process Manager — Control Systems

Projects
- Currently leading a project designing and implementing a full primary and secondary control system for a food manufacturing plant in the North West of England comprising 600 different processes and 50+ operators (project value £3.5m)
- Co-developed the process description for freight handling of the container terminal in Dover, followed by the implementation of a full scale safety control and tracking system for up to 10,000 containers yearly (total project value £45m)
- Redesign and implementation of whisky distillery to introduce 3 new intermediate process steps and enhance control systems throughout.
- Feasibility studies into new product developments

Responsibilities
- Leading a team of up to 5 people in operations and development of new product specific control software
- Responsible for costing and budgeting projects of up to £700k and managing company resources

2001-05   **Peugeot S.A.**   Barcelona, Spain

Business Process Analyst — Internal Project Management/IT

- Quickly came to represent the interface between senior management, operations & IT, playing a key role in all process, IT updates and implementations

Projects
- Played a decision making role in adapting the dated business process and billing software resulting in simplified operator tasks and process efficiency. Introduced/adapted new services in automation, stock handling and raw material purchasing.
- Company liaison and representative with business software providers during the procurement process including offer evaluation, and application specification
- Co-implemented Activity Based Costing tool defining operational drivers as well as cost pools and relationships between these
- Other smaller projects included introduction of monthly reporting for KPIs, development of a Sales-Information-Tool and management of master data

EDUCATION

Aug. 1998 to Jul. 2002	**King's College London**	Engineering	London, UK
Aug. 1994 to Jun. 1998	**Ecole Secondaire Paris**	Baccalaureat	Paris, France
Sep. 1985 to May 1994	**French Lycee Madrid**		Madrid, Spain

LANGUAGES, SKILLS AND INTERESTS

- Fluent in Spanish, French and English as well as proficient in German. Some Portuguese
- Programming skills in multiple computer programming languages, high degree of analytic and implementation experience

Visit **Vault Europe's Consulting Career Channel** at **www.Vault.com/Europe** for insider firm profiles, employee surveys of consultants in Europe, job listings, expert consulting career advice, insider salary information and more.

V∆ULT   CAREER LIBRARY   55

Schmoozing: Building and Maintaining a Network

Good networking skills are important throughout your career, but these skills are immensely helpful in opening doors with your favourite firms. You need to work especially hard at networking in a difficult economic climate, as a contact typically goes a lot further than a blind e-mail.

Generating a network from nothing

Firms don't recruit at all campuses. That's why schmoozing is even more crucial. Find a contact within the firms you are targeting, be it an alumnus, a colleague who worked there prior to university, your mother's best friend, or anyone else. If you truly have no contacts, then go ahead and call up the recruiter listed on the company's website, identify yourself, and express your interest in the firm.

You could then ask the contact for an informational interview. An informational interview is just that — a short discussion to gather more information about the firm. It can take place in person (which is preferable) or on the phone. Use the informational interview for two purposes — to get an "in" on the recruiting process and to learn more about the company prior to your interviews. Asking for an informational interview is often a more innocuous approach than asking for a regular interview outright. If you can't get an informational interview with a consultant in person, try for one over the phone. Firms aren't always looking for new employees, but most are always interested in selling their firm to others and generating publicity and goodwill.

Managing your contacts

We all have friends who just seem to know everyone. They know what others are up to and are a great resource for the best parties in town. They make networking and schmoozing look easy. But networking is hard, even for them. It takes a lot of effort to maintain a contact.

The key to networking is consistent follow-up. After a great conversation, you need to make sure you've locked an impression of yourself in that person's mind. A quick e-mail is an easy and acceptable way to do this. Simply re-introduce yourself, remind them of a few key things you talked about, and thank them again for their time. If someone did something particularly nice for you (like introduced you to a partner with special expertise in your area of interest), send him or her a thank-you note.

Continue to check in with your contacts throughout the process, especially if they are consultants. While it's great to stay in touch with the human resources staff because they manage the recruiting process, an endorsement by someone already working in the firm goes a long way. There is no real science to how often to call your contacts; your goal is to stay on the firm's radar without being overaggressive. Twice a month should be fine.

Good networkers also think ahead to when they might want to get in touch with the person next. For example, if the closed interview list deadline is next month, pencil in a day to call up your favourite contact at the firm for advice on the covering letter. Perhaps they will remember you and call the recruiting consultants to recommend you as someone with strong potential. In general, the more people you know in a particular organisation, the greater your chances of success.

Notes for on-campus recruiting

If you have a strong on-campus recruiting programme at your university, you're in luck. Make sure you attend the appropriate company presentations — you may be asked whether you attended the presentations at your interview, and in any case it's a great way to make contacts. (Here's one hint — approach consultants before the presentation when they have time, rather than after the presentation when they are sure to be mobbed.) Be sure to get from your career services office a list of all of the recruiting consulting companies, the date and time of their on-campus information session, the dates of the first round interviews, and the names of the appropriate contacts. Build a spreadsheet or list of target companies with all of this information so you can keep track of the process.

Most firms offer an information session where partners deliver an overview presentation of the firm and you can speak with current consultants. We strongly recommend you attend this session. You will be able to confirm your overall impression of the firm and its specific application process, and it's a great way to generate nominal contacts at each firm. Definitely try to speak with the current consultants and ask about what they do on the job and how they like it, and don't forget to get the business card of those you felt you connected with. If you spoke with someone for a long time, a good technique is to follow up with an e-mail to thank them for their time. You can then call with further questions. (Tip: these sessions often offer free food and cocktails. Even though it's free, don't go overboard! Trust us; the firms really remember those who do.)

In some European cities, the recruiting sessions of larger consultancies are not done on campus but in off-site locations, and all universities in the region receive invitations to make their students aware of the events. These sessions often take place in hotels and are

Visit **Vault Europe's Consulting Career Channel** at www.Vault.com/Europe for insider firm profiles, employee surveys of consultants in Europe, job listings, expert consulting career advice, insider salary information and more.

V/\ULT   CAREER LIBRARY   **57**

informative and good for building your network--but beware, competition between candidates is often even stiffer than in on-campus events, and you are likely to be one of many rather than one of the few. Make sure you arrive early and get some time with one of the consultants, although you will often find that it is mighty difficult to have a one-on-one conversation in this environment.

Other thoughts on schmoozing

Schmoozing involves more than just networking. When networking, you seek out people to help you on a single mission, without necessarily considering your ability to help them. Schmoozing, on the other hand, involves developing longer-term relationships for both parties' benefit. You begin these relationships with the goal of seeking a mutually beneficial outcome. You find people with whom you can exchange ideas, favours, and politics. Through schmoozing, you find people who will support you even when you do not need it. They actively become involved in your life, and vice versa.

Extroverts generally find schmoozing easier, because approaching strangers comes more naturally to them. Introverts are more selective about whom they approach. Either way, think of schmoozing as a lifestyle you constantly want to improve. The more relationships you develop, the more fruitful you will find your career.

Applying to the Firm

Now the fun part: the actual application.

Writing the covering letter

Firms vary on the importance of the covering letter. Some recruiters don't read it and go straight to the CV. Others look at it as a true writing sample. Don't take any chances; take the covering letter seriously. However, regard the cover letter as an opportunity. Use it to communicate things that do not come across in your CV and that you think will round up your image.

There are some standard components to covering letters in consulting. We aren't recommending that you follow this outline slavishly, but we do think you should include them all in some form:

• **Introduction** — Identify your current position or university standing, and express your general interest in the firm.

• **Relevant experience** — Discuss how your background and experience fits consulting. If the firm has a specialty, explain how and why you are interested in that specialty.

• **Interest in consulting** — Discuss (briefly) what aspects of consulting appeal to you. Is it the problem-solving? The variety? Your love of assisting clients?

• **Interest in the firm** — Why do you want to work for this firm?

• **Additional information** — Depending on the preference of the company, you may need to include information such as your preferred start date and office location. Be sure to list more than one office location if possible, because some firms have office-specific recruiting needs and you might increase your chances of getting employed if you list more than one office.

• **Next steps** — If you are applying through your university, the next steps are usually clear. (On campus, the recruiter will normally invite selected students to interview; some universities have a lottery system for interviews as well. If you are unfamiliar with how interviewers are assigned at your university, contact your career advisor.) Otherwise, you will need to specify the next form of contact. We suggest you write in your letter that you will follow up with the recruiter in a few days to discuss what happens next.

• **Closing** — Be sure to thank the reader for his or her consideration and time.

Visit **Vault Europe's Consulting Career Channel** at www.Vault.com/Europe for insider firm profiles, employee surveys of consultants in Europe, job listings, expert consulting career advice, insider salary information and more.

VAULT CAREER LIBRARY **59**

Is Consulting For You?

By Hannah Im

Why are potential consultants attracted to the field? Most often, their reasons include prestige, high pay, interesting work, travel opportunities, and peer pressure. Many such potential consultants are considering other fields, trying to decide if they would rather be consultants or investment bankers or marketing managers or the like. But potential consultants rarely consider whether they would be a good fit for the consulting field. Here, I try to explain some of the pressures and issues of being a consultant.

Not as easy as it looks

Consulting is not an easy job. More to the point, it is not a predictable job. There is no set routine. Each firm, each office, each practice/business line, and each client is different. And the travelling is not as glamorous as it sounds – it is, for me, the most gruelling part of the job, because it is so physically and mentally taxing – especially after the September 11 attacks.

With each client, I have to start from the bottom and convince them I am credible and can add value to their business. Some of my projects last only a few weeks, which makes it even more difficult to persuade them. Many times, they only decided to hire consultants as a last resort, because circumstances have become unmanageable. That means I'm always walking into a less-than-ideal situation from the first day. Clients spend a lot of money for consulting services and are not forgiving of the slightest faults in judgment, and they always want more than what they hired us to do in the first place.

Hours are consistent only in their inconsistency. One too many days have turned into later-than-late nights. And there's internal competition too. My colleagues in the past have included Olympic athletes, FBI agents, politicians, former CEOs and a nationally acclaimed investigative journalist. These are people with tremendous talent, vision and resources. They are also very competitive people who constantly seek to outdo each other and me.

Additionally, I am exposed to so much confidential information at my client sites that I am often faced with very difficult ethical choices. Some of these choices are not so easy to make – a lot of times, they end up being the "lesser of two evils."

The "WIFM" (a.k.a., What's In It For Me?)

Burnout is a big problem in our field. Many days I wake up wondering how being a consultant will make a difference in the larger scheme of life. God knows I would be a significantly happier person if I were a concert pianist. I suppose God also knows I am wrong to think so; otherwise, I would have been born with some modicum of musical talent.

I am in no way the world's greatest consultant, but I know my clients appreciate my involvement in their businesses. I am repeatedly asked back by clients for new projects, and a number have even written letters of gratitude to my employers. So I know I am a "lifer." I know how much satisfaction I have in helping my clients identify their inefficiencies, vulnerabilities, risks and unnoticed implications. I know how much more satisfied I am when I help my clients develop solutions and workable strategies. And I know that these efforts will result in a better company, which in turn means a better economy, especially when the client has a large market share in industries that can significantly impact the GDP. While I might not be affecting social policies, legislations, or paradigms, I know the work I do makes a difference for employees at those companies.

Hannah Im has been a consultant throughout her career. She specialises in business operations, specifically process improvement/reengineering and risk management. She has served as a consulting career expert for the Vault Consulting Career Channel at www.vault.com/europe.

Be sure to proof read; we've all heard stories of covering letters to Accenture that begin, "I'm very interested in a position with Bain and Company." This actually happens more often than you think at the undergraduate and MBA level. Students often apply to up to 20 companies at once, so there's a high chance of a mistake slipping through the cracks.

Triple-check everything. The consulting market is so competitive that the slightest error may sink your application. You may want to have a friend read your covering letters too.

Most of all, keep the covering letter to one page. It takes a lot of effort to make the letter both concise and powerful, and it will be worth the effort.

Additional materials

Most firms only want to see the covering letter and CV, but you should confirm that they don't have any special requirements. You will want to check what other requirements specific firms have for your CV or covering letter, including GCSE subjects and grades and UCAS points on the CV or office preference in the covering letter. Ask the firm's recruiting manager for these details.

Visit **Vault Europe's Consulting Career Channel** at **www.Vault.com/Europe** for insider firm profiles, employee surveys of consultants in Europe, job listings, expert consulting career advice, insider salary information and more.

VAULT CAREER LIBRARY 61

Sending it in

More firms these days request that candidates apply by e-mail. This is fine. Most of the time, you can send the covering letter as e-mail text and attach your CV in Microsoft Word format. We advise you to confirm this format with your recruiter contact.

Other firms will still demand CV and covering letter in digital form, but will make this part of an online application form. Nowadays, consultancies often use online application forms to better manage the large number of applicants they receive. Consulting is a popular choice of profession, and applicants are plentiful.

The online application form will include a selection of personal details like degrees and previous work experience as well as location preferences, some of which will overlap with information in your CV. Don't despair, this makes the selection process easier for the human resources department, which can then just query the database to find suitable candidates.

If you need to send a paper version, print your materials on nicely-woven CV paper stock using a laser printer. Paper clips are preferred to staples.

Following up

It is generally a good idea to check in with the recruiter and make sure your application was received. A quick e-mail is fine and will do the trick. If you entered your information into an online form, you will receive an automatic reply to your email confirming the reception. Campus recruiters are usually good about responding, because they know that the process is stressful.

Most firms have "core" universities they prioritise. If you are not from one of those core universities, or if you have already graduated, you will often have a more difficult time hearing back from the companies of your choice. Don't give up — keep contacting the firm if you are truly interested. Consulting firms appreciate polite persistence.

Differences in CV formats in other European countries

There is no right way of writing a CV but there are plenty of wrong ways. This is especially true if you consider the immense differences that exist between different countries in terms of what is required for a application. Even though the larger consultancies are making great strides in homogenising the application process across their single regional offices, it may still vary considerably. The only thing that seems to apply to all countries is the fact that a cover letter and CV are to be included.

Germans have the most cumbersome application, in form of what is called a "Bewerbungsmappe," including not only cover letter and CV but also copies of all relevant degrees and recommendations. The CV itself is to be kept factual, but can cover 2-3 pages if need be with a picture required (wear a tie). Special folders exist for these applications, which often end up stacking up to a small book with a few dozen pages.

In the UK the process is particularly easy. A CV and cover letter will often suffice, as degrees and recommendations are submitted once an offer is received. The CV should be kept as short as possible, with one side being the standard but two sides not frowned upon.

In Spain, CVs and covers are included together with copies of the degrees and recommendations, but less formally bound than in Germany. In Italy the process is similar to Spain, but recommendations carry more importance. Again France is similar, with firms often demanding complete documentation but without the formal binding.

It has to be noted, however, that consulting firms are increasingly demanding applicants to fill in their standard online application form, which is helping to iron out the differences between different countries. But beware, you will still be required to attach your CV in Microsoft Word or PDF format, so make sure it looks neat and fits the standards of the country you are applying to.

Visit **Vault Europe's Consulting Career Channel** at **www.Vault.com/Europe** for insider firm profiles, employee surveys of consultants in Europe, job listings, expert consulting career advice, insider salary information and more.

VAULT CAREER LIBRARY   63

The Interview

CHAPTER 5

What to Expect in the Interview

If all goes well, you will land a few interviews. The following is a typical format for the consulting interview process:

- 1st round: One or two half-hour interviews with a senior consultant. Expect at least one of these interviews to contain a case.

- 2nd round: Up to four 45-minute interviews. You can expect that all of these will be case interviews. At least one of these interviews probably will be with a partner, as many firms will not hire a candidate unless partners have spoken with the candidate. Most firms extend offers after the second round. If the candidate has requested a specific office, the interviews will most likely take place in that office. Otherwise, the candidate will interview at the nearest regional office or in a hotel. Although this is not often the case, you might be interviewing for a position based in Rome while in the London office.

- 3rd round: In rare cases, firms will ask candidates back for a third round of interviews, often exclusively with partners of the firm.

Consulting interviews fall into two types: the behavioral interview and the case/problem interview. The former determines the extent to which you fit the consultant profile and the firm's culture. The latter tests your problem solving skills and displays your thinking patterns to the interviewer. To an extent, both types of interviews also reveal how well you deal with stressful real-time challenges. Candidates at the undergraduate level might receive brainteasers and "guessestimates" instead of cases. MBA and advanced degree candidates typically are not asked directly to solve a brainteaser or do a guesstimate, though an estimate of industry market size might appear within a case. For more case interview practice, please refer to *The Vault Guide to the Case Interview* and the *Vault Case Interview Practice Guide*, available on the Vault web site and both online and traditional bookstores.

Visit **Vault Europe's Consulting Career Channel** at **www.Vault.com/Europe** for insider firm profiles, employee surveys of consultants in Europe, job listings, expert consulting career advice, insider salary information and more.

V∧ULT CAREER LIBRARY 65

The Resume/Behavioral Interview

Interviewers first want to determine if you have the "mental horsepower" (brains) and "quantitative and analytical ability" (math and logic skills) to be an asset. You must also be able to think "out of the box" (creatively) to come up with innovative ideas and approaches.

While your CV provides structure for the interview, be sure your side of the conversation provides more than a regurgitation of the CV's key points. Focus on the same skills you underscored in your CV, but use different examples of teamwork, leadership, confidence, and technical skills. Show them that the examples on your CV do not constitute the entirety of your abilities and make the interview interesting for your interviewer by telling relevant anecdotes. Interviewers take on the responsibility of shaping their firm's culture and/or ensuring compliance with firm standards. Generally, consulting firms want smart, ambitious, hardworking, dedicated and analytical people with pleasant demeanours.

During the interview, pay attention to what you say and how you say it. Listen carefully to the questions. Too many people lose points by answering the questions incorrectly, incompletely or inappropriately. Make your answers logical and structured. Provide relevant examples. Speak in complete sentences, and do not go off on tangents or trail off midway through a sentence. Also, watch your fillers: "you know," "um" and "like." Ensure that you speak eloquently.

Some specific skills and qualities that interviewers look for:

- Leadership skills, to lead consulting and client teams and to promote your ideas
- Teamwork, to work with other consultants, clients and vendors toward solutions
- Analytical skills, to crunch numbers and work through information in a logical manner
- Presentation skills, to communicate findings to fellow consultants and clients alike
- Creativity, to solve problems and think "out of the box"
- Thick skin, for those times when your work is criticized
- Personality and sense of humor, to diffuse stressful situations

During your interviews, remember these specific points:

- Never express uncertainty or insecurity about your skills or give the interviewer any reason to question your confidence or abilities.
- Refrain from revealing your dislike for travel or your attachment to home.
- Avoid getting defensive or sensitive when answering tough questions, including: "What people do you have trouble getting along with?" Another favorite: "Tell us about your shortcomings."

During your interview, be prepared for some version of the "airplane test." The interviewer imagines sitting next to you on an eight-hour flight across the Atlantic. She or he decides which is more preferable: Conversing with you for more than 30 seconds or faking sleep throughout the whole flight to avoid you altogether. To pass the test, show genuine interest in something outside the business realm or crack a joke. Just be sure to choose a topic that presents you as mature, insightful and interesting and make certain that the topic is tasteful, amusing and non-controversial.

Behavioral Questions

Consulting firms use "behavioral interview questions" to measure "softer" attributes. Behavioral interview questions ask you to reveal how you behaved in particular situations, be it at work or in a personal situation. Firms using behavioral interviews believe a candidate's responses reveal a lot about personality and skills. They also believe the firm can project future behavioral patterns based on the past. Some consulting firms use behavioral questions almost to the exclusion of more traditional consulting case questions. To prepare, practice answering the more frequently asked behavioral questions until you can answer them smoothly.

Practice Behavioral Interview Questions

When asking behavioral questions, your interviewer first listens to your answers at face value and then assesses your thinking process (ingesting the question, processing the answer, assembling the words, and presenting the answer). They also use their assessment to project the likelihood of your success as a consultant. Be aware that these questions do not often represent a separate section of the interview but will be interspersed all along the interview often as a reaction to a situation you describe in your CV.

1. How do you deal with someone in your group who isn't pulling his or her weight, or disagrees with your goals?

Avoid criticism. Try to think of a time when you encouraged someone to do his or her best or won someone over to your side. Team sports examples are good here. Emphasize how everyone has something to contribute.

2. What position do you normally take on a team?

Avoid portraying yourself as an obsequious follower or a tyrannical dictator. Consulting firms want people (especially neophytes) who ask questions, make contributions, and get their points across. They want someone who neither passively receives information nor commandeers the entire case team.

3. Tell me what you're most proud of on your resume.

Choose something that conveys the qualities consulting firms want and that lets you explain something not obvious to the interviewer. (Because many consulting firms have international branches, discussing a study abroad programme or an international position might win you points.) A stay abroad demonstrates not only that you are keen to broaden your horizons, but can also serve as proof of command of a foreign language (often English).

4. How have you shown leadership in the past?

Consulting firms like candidates who show strong managerial potential, and they like to see evidence of your leadership skills. Speak of leadership roles you took during college, such as co-chair of a fund-raising event.

Many aspiring consultants have not had specific leadership roles. If you have work experience, describe a time you took initiative, such as created a training programme for junior team members or convinced the management to switch from an outdated version of Windows to Linux. If you haven't, talk about proactive efforts you made in your student groups. The point is to show initiative; past leadership positions are a proxy for this, but you will do just as well by describing key experiences.

Military service, common in some European countries, can serve as a leadership experience.

5. Why have you chosen to interview at our firm?

Consulting involves a lot of research. Show off your skills here. Explain your interest in a strategy firm (or change management, or whatever), and relate your interest to what you know of the firm. Include what you want to gain from the firm and what you believe you can contribute. State why the firm stands in a good position to accomplish your goals and how the firm can benefit from your contributions. Demonstrate your abilities to weave data from separate sources into a single analysis.

6. What is the worst mistake you've ever made?

Do not cite an egregious lapse in judgment along the lines of: "It was really stupid of me to jump bail." Instead, describe a valuable lesson you learned (preferably some time ago). Remember to include your lesson and why the lesson holds value to you even today. "I remember when I didn't fully research buying a car, and I ended up buying a car that looked good but cost me thousands in repairs. I'll never fail to do my homework again."

7. Why should we not hire you?

Leave out any actual flaws unknown to your interviewer. Instead, explain why something that looks like a weakness actually represents a strength (or at best, something neutral). "I can understand that you would potentially be put off by my lack of economics and business coursework. But I think my sales experience and my score of 80% on the maths portion of my finals should alleviate those concerns."

Visit **Vault Europe's Consulting Career Channel** at **www.Vault.com/Europe** for insider firm profiles, employee surveys of consultants in Europe, job listings, expert consulting career advice, insider salary information and more.

VAULT   CAREER LIBRARY   69

The Case Interview

Consulting interviewers use interview questions to test your analytical ability, reasoning skills, confidence, and knowledge of business concepts. Case interviews simulate live scenarios to test your mind's quickness and confirm the skills you claim on your resume. You must discuss hypothetical situations based on information provided to you and make assumptions based on commonly-known facts. Even if you have no background knowledge of the case, you must still address the question thoughtfully under pressure. The interviewer cares more about how you arrived at your answer than if you answer correctly, so be sure to explain your thought process too.

Case interview questions fall into three broad categories: business cases, guesstimates, and brainteasers.

Business cases

If you are interviewing with a strategy consulting firm, count on plenty of cases during the interview process. Put very simply, case interviews are problem-solving exercises. While some interviewers draw on recent real-world experience to develop a case, you are not expected to have any industry knowledge. The interviewer is more interested in checking out your thought process and assessing your analytical ability, creativity, and poise. Some companies present cases as written documents to be read and prepared. But usually, the interviewer describes the key facts and issues of the case before asking the candidate for an analysis. Several firms (e.g., Monitor and Accenture) ask you to solve a case as part of a team with other job candidates.

The case usually consists of a business scenario and a question about it. For example: "A foreign company with extra cash on hand wants to enter the American fast food market. What would you tell them?" While every case is different, follow the tips below to improve your chances of cracking it without too much difficulty.

Some quick case tips

• Before jumping into an answer, ask the interviewer a number of questions to gather vital information about the case. Your interviewer will answer you with pieces of information to help you formulate new questions and, ultimately, your case recommendations. (At the same time, avoid tiring your interviewer and recognise when you have asked enough questions. If your interviewer starts repeating himself or herself or says something like, "You should be able to give me an answer," stop asking questions.)

- One interviewee cautions: "Consulting firms are looking for people who will think carefully before answering; this is very important in the case interview. Don't say the first thing that comes to your mind, even if you're certain about it. If you're trying to choose between appearing to be slow and appearing to be a cocky idiot, choose the former."

- Ask about best practices in the industry. Find out what other companies in this industry do when facing similar issues.

- Avoid making assumptions without checking them with the interviewer, or at the very least, state that you are making an assumption. If your case concerns a major vehicle manufacturer, you might mistakenly assume the client is General Motors, Ford or Toyota, when it is actually JCB.

- After gathering all the information you think you need, start formulating your recommendations. If you like using standard frameworks, remember to use the appropriate one. Run the framework through your mind to ensure you are not forgetting a vital area of analysis. For instance, the Porter's Five Forces model might help you analyse a market situation and identify all of the areas of potential threat. Based on the model, you can recommend the company's market strategy.

- If you are unfamiliar with frameworks, state so and proceed as logically as you are able. Voice your analysis — why and how you come to your questions and conclusions is also important.

- After giving your recommendations, consider pointing out possible flaws and assumptions in your thinking. If it's clear you really didn't do well on the case, you might try explaining how you would have approached it differently given the chance.

- Speak and reason aloud during your case interview. Your thought process is more important than your ultimate conclusions; your interviewer must hear your reasoning and the logical steps you are taking to reach your conclusions.

- Always bring paper and a reliable pen with you to any consulting interview. You might want to take notes during the case interview (and for any guesstimates or quantitative brainteasers your interviewer might throw at you). Asking your interviewer for paper and a pen during the interview gives the impression that you are disorganised and unprepared.

- Everyone gets stuck in a case interview at some point. One tactic is to simply admit you are stuck and try thinking out loud through the problem again. "I don't seem to be getting anywhere with this line of thinking, so I'm going to start again and think through things from the beginning." You can also just ask your interviewer for help: "I have a lot of

Visit **Vault Europe's Consulting Career Channel** at www.Vault.com/Europe for insider firm profiles, employee surveys of consultants in Europe, job listings, expert consulting career advice, insider salary information and more.

VAULT CAREER LIBRARY 71

good information in front of me, but I seem to be running into a dead end here. Maybe you could help me talk through the problem." These alternatives are both a lot better than staying silent; after all, this is exactly what would happen if you were working on a real project together and you needed help.

• No matter what, never show any signs of being flustered in a case interview. Remember to breathe! Your composure before your client (or lack thereof) is a key factor of your evaluation.

Your Experience, Your Advantage

In some cases the interviewer will direct the attention towards your own field of expertise during case studies in an attempt to gain more information about you. If case studies and/or guesstimates are not predetermined, the interviewer may choose to give you a topic you are very familiar with and assess your ability to keep the 'big picture' in mind.

On some occasions, the interviewer will have some knowledge about the industry thanks to previous projects in the sector, but often he/she will draw on the general consulting experience to quiz you about the industry.

In such cases, be forthcoming with your knowledge and impressions without being too opinionated, providing excessive detail or too much anecdotal evidence. Be balanced and factual and try to use your knowledge to your full advantage. The interviewer is assessing your understanding of the environment, ability to keep the 'big picture' in mind and your skill to communicate complex topics.

This is a great opportunity to shine so play it to your best advantage.

Sample Qualitative Case Questions

> **1) A major film entertainment company wants us to assist them in building a distribution network for home video. They want to know whether they should build their own distribution network or continue to contract with third parties.**

Start by asking your interviewer some basic questions:

• What are other entertainment companies doing?

• What are the current costs?

• Does the company have the staff and resources to create its own distribution network?

• Of the major entertainment companies producing videos, do most distribute through their proprietary supply chains or through third parties?

• What is the client's current cost of distribution through its contractual partner(s)?

• Has the client considered building its own distribution network before retaining us? If so, what were its findings?

• Does the client have a dedicated functional staff assigned to the project? If so, what functional areas do they represent?

After establishing some basic facts, ask more detailed questions. Your interviewer might allude to certain avenues to discuss or shut down others. If the interviewer confirms the company has enough staff to handle setting up its network, stop delving into the ramifications of reassigning personnel.

If, through questioning, you decide staying with a third-party distributor makes the most sense, ask the next logical question: Should the company stay with its current distributor or choose a new one?

• Who are possible alternative partners? Who uses them?

• Could you characterise the relationship between the client's distribution partner and the client? Is there a possibility of retaliation on the part of the distribution partner if the client severs its ties to this party?

• How many weeks of supply are currently in the distribution partner's pipeline?

Visit **Vault Europe's Consulting Career Channel** at www.Vault.com/Europe for insider firm profiles, employee surveys of consultants in Europe, job listings, expert consulting career advice, insider salary information and more.

V/\ULT CAREER LIBRARY **73**

• How receptive are the client's accounts to changing distribution partners? Has a value proposition been created to show that a client-owned supply chain would be more efficient or valuable to the accounts?

• Does the client have any financial interest in the distribution partner that might have to be severed?

When you feel ready, make a recommendation. You might be asked a more qualitative case question as well. (Recruiting insiders tell Vault that undergraduates and graduate candidates without MBAs are more likely to receive qualitative cases.) Qualitative business cases determine if you can discuss a company intelligently and analytically and use business concepts and terminology naturally in conversation.

> **2) We've seen a lot of consolidation in the pharmaceuticals industry over the last ten years. What factors do you think drive this activity?**

You don't have to know anything about the pharmaceutical industry or even companies like Pfizer or GlaxoSmithKline to do well with this question. On the other hand, you want to show that you can think through a complex industry using some basic analytic thinking. (Still, we recommend that you read *The Financial Times* or the local financial newspaper on a daily basis in the weeks before your interviews.)

If you are unfamiliar with the pharmaceutical industry — and if you are, you can say so to your interviewer without penalty — ask some questions to orient yourself. What exactly do pharmaceutical companies make? How large is the industry? How do products originate? Are there a few major players or is the industry more fragmented? How do consumers choose among different drugs that offer a similar treatment?

At a very high level, you should be able to ascertain or confirm the following pieces of information:

• Pharmaceutical companies develop and market drugs that help people with a wide variety of medical conditions, such as cancer, influenza, or nasal congestion.

• Given the recent consolidation, the industry is dominated by several large players. The list includes Pfizer, GlaxoSmithKline, and Bristol-Myers Squibb.

• Market research suggests that direct-to-consumer ads have been fairly effective. Consumers are indeed requesting prescription drugs and purchasing over-the-counter drugs on the basis of advertising.

• All new drugs undergo several expensive stages of testing before they can come to market.

• Few drugs pass all phases of testing. Successful drugs take many years (6-10) to complete the full cycle of testing.

• Drugs can be patented, but most patents expire in seventeen years. At this point, the drug will be subject to generic competitors. Many drugs are patented before the full cycle of testing finishes.

• While all of the major pharmaceutical companies have their own R&D departments, most partner with biotechnology companies, who specialise in the research and development of new life science technologies. Biotech firms usually restrict their attention to the discovery and pre-clinical stages of the R&D process, and the pharmaceutical companies carry the drug through the last stages of testing.

A good answer to this question might suggest that mergers are either revenue-enhancing or cost-reducing to the parties involved.

• Revenue-enhancing — One company might buy another because it wants access to a larger revenue base. When its patent expires, a drug becomes subject to generic competitors, and the drug will make less money for its parent company. This is why drug companies are constantly on the prowl for new drugs to develop.

• Cost-reducing — A big reason for pharma companies to merge is to save costs. Many companies save money by combining overhead and R&D expenses and reducing headcount. Sales and marketing are enormous expenditures for pharma companies.

An even better answer would incorporate some more advanced reasons.

• Mergers in the pharma industry can reduce risk because the combined drug pipeline will be larger. Very few drugs in the R&D stage pass the regulatory tests and make it to market. Each stage of testing (Phase I/II/III) has a historically low probability of success, so if one multiplies out the probabilities, there is a very low overall probability of success for any given drug. So, a pharma company wants to have as many products in development as possible to ensure that a few will make it to market and that perhaps one over a given timeframe will become a real hit.

• A company might want to capture the revenues from a competitor's winning drug. For example, Pfizer purchased Warner-Lambert mainly for its leading drug, Lipitor. Pfizer also made a bid to purchase Pharmacia largely because of Pharmacia's strength in oncology.

Visit **Vault Europe's Consulting Career Channel** at **www.Vault.com/Europe** for insider firm profiles, employee surveys of consultants in Europe, job listings, expert consulting career advice, insider salary information and more.

VAULT   CAREER LIBRARY   75

• Companies might also merge because of irrationality. Companies in the 1990's believed that scaling up was the way to go.

• Because marketing and brand awareness are so important, a larger pharma company can join two strong brand names with joint advertising and create an even larger market power than the two companies individually could have had before.

> **3) A restaurant owner is setting up a new restaurant and making some basic decisions on the layout. He is making a decision on the facilities to place in the toilets for customers to dry their hands. Initial research suggests that he has three options — paper towels, roller towels, and hot air dryers. He needs to decide today. What should he consider in his decision making process?**

In the initial analysis, ask a number of questions that will influence your decision.

• What type of restaurant is it going to be — luxury, moderate or cheap?

• How many customers does he expect? How many tables? Is it open during the day? In the evening?

• Has he done any customer research to see what customers would prefer?

Fairly soon in the process, start asking about the economics of the three options. Expect the interviewer to give you more information:

In the initial research, the restaurant owner found the following information from the suppliers of the drying facilities:

• Dryers have an initial cost of £500 each (but you need two — one for each lavatory) and a total monthly service charge of £100 per month. The supplier estimates that the lifetime of a drier is four years.

• Paper towels cost five cents each. The number of paper towels that you need varies directly with the number of customers you anticipate. So if you expect 50 customers a night, expect they will use 50 towels.

• Towelling rolls cost £5 per roll (and again, you need two — one for each restroom). The rolls are changed daily if there are more than 2,000 customers per month. They are changed every other day if there are less than 2,000 customers per month.

At this point, you know the option you select varies with the number of customers. Therefore, it makes sense to look at a break-even calculation. First of all, take the dryers. They cost £100 per month to operate, plus an upfront charge of £1,000 that depreciates over their lifetime (i.e. an additional £1,000/(4 x 12) per month = £21 per month). Therefore, their total cost is approximately £120 per month, which does not vary with the number of customers coming into the restaurant.

Secondly, look at the paper towels option. These vary directly with number of customers in the restaurant, at a cost of £0.05 per customer. Therefore, assuming few customers per month, paper towels are cheaper than dryers. Figure out how many customers have to come to the restaurant each month to make the dryers more cost effective. The cost of towels would have to exceed £120 per month, equating to 2,400 customers per month (£120/£0.05).

Determine if the rolls option affects this break-even amount. At less than 2,000 customers per month, the rolls cost £10 every other day or £150 per month (£10 x 15 days). This, in itself, costs more than both the dryer and the towels option. With more than 2,000 customers, it only looks less favourable. Therefore, the real economic decision is between towels and dryers. At less than 2,400 customers per month (or 2,400/30 = 80 customers per night), you prefer the towels. Once the number of customers increases above this, you recommend switching to dryers.

Following the economic analysis, drop a few non-economic questions that might sway the balance:

• Are there additional staff costs of cleaning up paper towel waste?

• How many suppliers of each option are there? If there is a single supplier, does he have the power to raise prices in the future?

Visit **Vault Europe's Consulting Career Channel** at www.Vault.com/Europe for insider firm profiles, employee surveys of consultants in Europe, job listings, expert consulting career advice, insider salary information and more.

VAULT CAREER LIBRARY

77

Guesstimates

In guesstimates, your interviewer generally asks you to estimate the market size for a product or service and observes your reasoning process. The key is not necessarily to get the right answer, but to show your ability to tackle a problem logically, approach assumptions sensibly, and perform simple calculations quickly without a calculator.

Guesstimate cracking tips

• For use in your analysis, assume the United Kingdom has 64 million people and 10 million businesses. (Consider rounding down to 60 million, as long as you inform your interviewer that you are doing so.)

• Make reasonable assumptions, with rounded, easy-to-work-with numbers (difficult numbers might throw off your calculations), and go from there.

• Remember that you are expected to use a pen and notepad to work through your calculations.

• If you don't know a number, like the population of Brazil or the circumference of the globe, ask for it. Avoid stumbling your way through an answer based on inaccurate assumptions.

• Talk through your steps aloud as you go through your calculations. This is the key to every guesstimate, so use this to impress with your clear train of thought

• Remember that guesstimates, like cases, also involve elements of creativity and problem solving. For example, when asked "How much change would you find on the floor of a shopping centre?" ask, "Is there a fountain in the shopping centre?"

Sample Guesstimate

1. How many gallons of white house paint are sold in the U.S. each year?

The "start big" approach

If unsure where to begin your analysis, start with the basic assumption that 270 million people live in the United States. If 270 million people live in the United States, perhaps half of them live in houses (or 135 million people). The average family size is about three, which measures out to 45 million houses in the United States. Add another 10 percent or so for second houses and houses used for other purposes besides residential. Conclude there are about 50 million houses.

If houses are painted every 10 years on average, then five million houses get painted every year. Assuming one gallon covers 100 square feet of wall and the average house has 2,000 square feet, each house needs twenty gallons. Therefore, 100 million gallons of paint are sold per year (five million houses times 20 gallons). (Note: If you want to be clever, ask your interviewer whether to include inner walls as well.) If 80 percent of all houses are white, then 80 million gallons of white house paint are sold each year. (Remember that last step!)

The "start small" approach

Take a town of 27,000 (about 1/10,000th of the population). If you use the same assumption that half the town lives in houses in groups of three, then there are 4,500 houses. Add another ten percent for good measure, and there are really 5,000 houses in your guesstimate. Painted every 10 years, 500 houses get painted in any given year. If each house has 2,000 square feet of wall, and each gallon covers 100 square feet, then each house needs 20 gallons. Therefore, 10,000 gallons of house paint are sold each year in your typical town. Perhaps 8,000 of those are white. Multiply by 10,000, and you have 80 million gallons.

If your interviewer asks you how you would actually get that number as a consultant, use your creativity — e.g., contact major paint producers or conduct a small sample of the second calculation in a few representative towns.

Visit **Vault Europe's Consulting Career Channel** at **www.Vault.com/Europe** for insider firm profiles, employee surveys of consultants in Europe, job listings, expert consulting career advice, insider salary information and more.

VAULT CAREER LIBRARY 79

More Sample Guesstimates

1. How many 747s are above England right now?

2. How much beer is consumed in the United Kingdom each year?

3. How many hair dressers are there in London?

4. How many petrol stations are there in Birmingham?

5. What is the annual size of the golf ball market in the Europe? What factors drive demand?

6. How many train stations are there in the UK?

Brainteasers

Brainteasers — or, as one disgruntled interviewee referred to them, "mind splitters" — are the genre of questions along the line of, "Why are manhole covers round?" Some brainteasers look more like logic problems, while others require more mathematics. Be forewarned — some of these questions are tricky, and it is possible you might not solve them in a short amount of time. Their main function is to test your courage under fire.

Keep your composure! Do not tell your interviewer that the brainteaser cannot be solved or is unreasonable. As a consultant, you will find yourself on the spot all the time, so your interviewer wants to ensure that you can keep your cool.

Visit **Vault Europe's Consulting Career Channel** at **www.Vault.com/Europe** for insider firm profiles, employee surveys of consultants in Europe, job listings, expert consulting career advice, insider salary information and more.

VAULT CAREER LIBRARY 81

Sample Brainteasers

1. You and a neighbour plan garage sales for the same day. You both plan to sell the same used TV model. You want to sell the TV for £100, but your neighbour insists on selling his for £40. What should you do?

Naturally, you think the right answer hinges on compromise — you sell your TV for more than £40 but something less than £100. But in the land of business, the right answer requires taking an underutilised asset and turning it around for profit maximisation. In this case, buy your neighbour's TV for £40 and then sell each TV for £100.

2. You stand in a room with three light switches. Each controls one of three light bulbs in the next room. You must figure out which switch controls which bulb. You have some limitations — you can flick only two switches and you may enter the room only once.

Consultants and clients alike love "out-of-the-box" thinking. Some suggest drilling a hole in the wall or calling a friend for assistance. One applicant suggested the switches might be dimmer switches — each light bulb could be set to a certain level of illumination, making solving the puzzle easy. One elegant solution, however, is to turn one light bulb on for 10 minutes and turn it off. Turn another bulb on and go into the room. The light bulb that is on clearly goes with the switch that you turned on last. Now feel the bulbs. The hot one was on recently.

3. Four men must cross a bridge in 17 minutes. The bridge is very narrow and only two men can cross at once. It is night-time, and whoever is crossing the bridge must carry a torch. Alan can cross in one minute, Bert in two, Cedric in five minutes, and Don in 10 minutes. The men crossing the bridge go at the pace of the slowest individual. How should they cross?

First, Alan and Bert cross together with the torch, which takes two minutes. Alan returns with the torch, which takes one minute. Three minutes have elapsed. Cedric and Don then cross with the torch, which takes ten minutes. At the 13-minute mark, Bert returns with the torch, taking two minutes. Bert and Alan go back across the bridge, for a total time elapsed of 17 minutes.

4. Why is a manhole cover round? (The classic brainteaser: Originally asked by Microsoft, this still makes the rounds among consulting and high-tech firms.)

There are many answers to this puzzler. A round manhole cover will not fall into a hole, making it safer. A round manhole cover can be rolled on its edge and will not cut anyone. Round covers also do not need to be rotated to fit over a hole.

Visit **Vault Europe's Consulting Career Channel** at **www.Vault.com/Europe** for insider firm profiles, employee surveys of consultants in Europe, job listings, expert consulting career advice, insider salary information and more.

VAULT CAREER LIBRARY 83

Practicing with Your Friends Before the Interview

Practice makes perfect

It is one thing to tear apart a business problem in the privacy of your own space. But it is an entirely different endeavour to walk through that analysis out loud for a complete stranger — someone who has done the analysis herself in the real world, someone who is prepared to challenge your thoughts and even be a bit antagonistic. How many of us have tried to explain a solution to someone else and stumbled on words, stuttered, threw in a few too many ums, or had to retrace our steps after losing our place? How to ensure that you are as eloquent as possible in the interview? Simple: practice makes perfect.

Smart candidates realise that the case interview is a fit interview in disguise. The interviewer is checking you for analytic aptitude. In addition, the interviewer is getting a sense of what it would be like to work with you. How good are you at communicating your logic? How would clients perceive you? What would you be like to work with on a team? It is just as important to practice the actual vocal delivery of the analysis as it is to be able to think through the analysis itself. Don't forget to smile once in a while!

We know of a handful of people who walked right into their first case interview and nailed it. But for most of us, the case interview can be a tougher communication proposition than public speaking. The better prepared you are to walk through your thinking aloud and explain your analysis in clear, succinct sentences, the better you will do at the real thing.

The good news is that you can learn to crack cases. The best way? Practice. Pair up with your friends, colleagues, or classmates. Have one person play the interviewer and the other person play the interviewee. The interviewer should read one of the sample cases beforehand, understand the analysis, and be prepared to guide the interviewee through the case. Make sure the interviewee hasn't read through the case ahead of time. The interviewer should then guide the interviewee through a mock interview. At the undergraduate level, include brainteasers and guesstimate questions in addition to a qualitative case. At the MBA level, you will want to use a slightly more complex business case.

After the questions, the interviewer might want to give the interviewee balanced feedback on his or her performance and go over the study notes. For example, you can score the interviewee's performance as follows:

- **Presentation** — Shook hands, smiled, was well-dressed and displayed solid manners and business etiquette throughout. Maintained eye contact throughout the interview. (10 points)

- **Communication** — Relayed thoughts and ideas to the interviewer clearly and succinctly. Explained thought processes in sufficient detail for the interviewer. (30 points)

- **Quantitative skills** — Showed good facility with numbers, including guesstimates (15 points)

- **Problem solving** — Followed a logical, thorough, well-connected path of reasoning to solve the answer. Laid out a road map upfront and continued to think out loud. Used a framework if appropriate. Showed the ability to be flexible and change directions if the interviewer wanted to guide the case a different way. (30 points)

- **Summary** — Wrapped up the case for the interviewer, bringing together the pieces of the puzzle and offering thoughtful recommendations and follow-up insights. (10 points)

- **Questions** — Asked the interviewer two or three thoughtful questions specific to the interviewer's firm. (5 points)

Of course, the actual breakdown will vary according to each firm you interview with. What will not change is the importance of how well you answer the questions, present yourself, and communicate your answer.

Best practices for practicing

Here are a few pointers to make sure you get the most out of your practice sessions.

1. Take it seriously.

If you are the interviewee, bring your leather notepad and favourite pen. Review the frameworks in this guide and apply them judiciously. Don't forget to take notes while the interviewer is speaking, and nod and paraphrase to demonstrate good listening. Above all, don't forget to answer the question.

If you are the interviewer, be realistic. Don't be overly willing to give up the answers or hints without being asked, but if the interviewee asks for some help, go ahead and give it..

2. Simulate the actual case interview format.

Here is the typical format for a case interview (this will, of course, vary depending on the firm):

(1) Direct fit or behavioral questions: why consulting? Why this firm? Why you? (5-10 minutes)

Visit **Vault Europe's Consulting Career Channel** at **www.Vault.com/Europe** for insider firm profiles, employee surveys of consultants in Europe, job listings, expert consulting career advice, insider salary information and more.

VAULT CAREER LIBRARY **85**

(2) Case questions (15-20 minutes)

(3) Questions for the interviewer (3-5 minutes)

Case interviews often start with a handful of behavioral interview questions, and almost all of the time they will fall in some form of the 3 basic questions in (1). The interviewee should have quick, thorough answers to these questions ready. Also, pretend the interviewer is from a specific consulting firm, and have the interviewee prepare a few questions to ask the interviewer at the end.

3. Focus on communication.

This is a great environment for the interviewee to practice communicating his or her analysis in a succinct, clear, engaging manner.

4. Practice with different types of people.

You never know what kind of personality your interviewer will have, and you don't want to get used to a certain case giver's style. Moreover, we tend to be a little more forgiving of our friends. Try practicing with people you don't know very well but who are willing to help you. These include current consultants, alumni of your university, career services employees or fellow students. Also, practice in front of the mirror; this will help you see yourself through the eyes of the interviewer and will help you practice the formulations you will later use in the real meeting.

Questions for the Interviewer

Every single consulting interview ends with an opportunity for the candidate to ask the interviewer a few questions about the firm. Some candidates come unprepared for this and have nothing to ask. Arrive prepared to ask a few questions of your interviewer. Many people underestimate the importance of this part of the interview section. Posing interesting and relevant questions is a big part of a consultant's day-to-day work!

Remember, you are evaluating the firm as well. What would you need to know in order to make your decision? Would you need to hear an honest answer about the travel load? Are you concerned about the firm's early requirement of industry specialisation? Before your interview, take a few minutes and think through what key questions you must have answered. If you won't work anywhere that won't let you transfer to the San Francisco office in two years, you'd better ask!

Interview Questions That Never Get Asked (But Are Always Answered)

Consultants will look for anything that resembles poor personal skills in the screening process. We know far too many anecdotes of people with great consulting skills shooting themselves in the foot by not taking care of the basics, such as grooming and etiquette.

In addition to the usual interview questions, consultants are looking to answer three implicit questions about each of the people they interview. Make sure you give your interviewer the right answers to these questions.

• **Does this person really want to work here?** Does he or she seem genuinely enthusiastic about the consulting industry and, specifically, this firm? Did this person care enough to look the part or throw on a suit and run out the door? Did this person show up on time? Did this person ask thoughtful questions at the end of the interview?

• **Could I put this person in front of the client?** The interviewer is assessing your professionalism. He or she wants to find out if you would be a solid representative of the firm to the client. Your speech is especially important; if you are too nervous or not eloquent, the interviewer may doubt your ability to run or participate in a meeting or interview.

• **Would I want to work with this person?** Recall the "airplane test." The interviewer wants to hire someone likeable, someone with whom he or she could work late into the

Visit **Vault Europe's Consulting Career Channel** at www.Vault.com/Europe for insider firm profiles, employee surveys of consultants in Europe, job listings, expert consulting career advice, insider salary information and more.

VAULT CAREER LIBRARY 87

night, wait in an airport, drive to the client or share a meal. A decent sense of humour and the all-important spark of energy should be there as well. In other words, the interviewer is deciding if he or she would want you on the same project team.

How does an interviewer answer these questions? The following sections cover aspects of the interview that help answer them. These issues may seem so fundamental that attention need not be paid to them, but in some ways these presentation elements are the most important aspects of your consulting interview.

Asking Questions During the Interview

You are through the thick of your interview. You have explained in great detail why you went to that school and how you ended up at that university, what your interests are and maybe even shared a few anecdotes with your interviewer. It is now your turn to to ask the questions as the interviewer offers to answer anything you might ask.

This is a key moment in any interview as it not only represents an opportunity for you to learn about the company you are applying to, but also gives you the chance to make a further impression by asking interesting and relevant questions. Asking good questions demonstrates not only that you have been doing your research but also that the interest you have in the company is genuine. Relevant questions will leave a lasting impression with the interviewer; bland questions will be a missed opportunity. Remember that questions are normally asked at the end of interviews and therefore are the last opportunity to shine!

So apart from asking what the typical day in the life of a person in your position would look like, think of slightly more cunning ways of gaining some insight.

Sample questions:

1. Can you tell me what you are working on at present?
2. What is the best thing and the worst thing about your job?
3. If you were able to change anything in the company, what would this be?
4. Do you usually work on one or more things at a time?
5. How do you support employee development?
6. What was the most interesting and the most boring case you have worked on?

Dress the part

There's no reason to max out your credit cards on the swankiest of Armani suits. Still, presentation is important. It speaks to your interest in the firm and the impression you will make on clients.

How should you dress for interviews? Even though consultants are shifting to business casual in the office and on client sites, interview protocol hasn't changed that much. Unless specifically told otherwise, stick with business formal in the interview. Men should wear a pressed dark suit, clean shirt, tie, belt, dark socks, and polished dark shoes. (Bonus points for those gentlemen who successfully match the belt with the shoes.) Women should wear a dark suit (either trouser or skirt), a blouse or coordinating crew-neck sweater, tights, and nice shoes (either heels or flat). Dress as if you are already a consultant with the firm.

Eccentricities bear risks as some interviewers might deem them as unprofessional, so be careful what you choose to wear. Look yourself over before you head out the door and make sure you don't have any "negative distractions." These include things like ripped tights and untied shoes. One candidate was an Oxbridge first class student with great leadership experience and terrific problem-solving skills. He interviewed with a leading IT consultancy and had a great interview; the interviewer was visibly impressed that he had nailed the case, and the two had good rapport. Smiling, the young man went home, stopped in the bathroom, and was horrified to see that one of the two buttons on his shirt collar was unattached. It was a small thing, but it looked very sloppy. The message on his answering machine the next day informed him that he wouldn't be called back for the second round. While he never confirmed if the shirt collar did him in, he wonders to this day if that was the reason he didn't make it. Again, it's about reflecting that you cared enough to take care of the easy details. (On some level, the interviewer might extrapolate such details to how careful you would be with your Excel spreadsheet.)

What to bring

We mentioned before that you should bring a pad and a reliable pen. Another companion for consulting interviews should be a leather or high-quality vinyl folder that holds a single letter-sized notepad. Here's what you should put in it:

- **Clean pad of paper** — It doesn't have to be graph paper, but it should be something you feel comfortable working out problems on.

- **Pen or pencil** — Test it out beforehand! Although most interviewers will provide you with one, the horror stories about interviewees asking their interviewer for a pen exist for

Visit **Vault Europe's Consulting Career Channel** at www.Vault.com/Europe for insider firm profiles, employee surveys of consultants in Europe, job listings, expert consulting career advice, insider salary information and more.

VAULT CAREER LIBRARY

89

a reason. Remember that you will likely be using this device for note taking and calculations, so bring your favourite instrument. And bring a spare.

- **Turn off your mobile phone**

- **A few extra copies of your CV** — Your interviewer will likely have a copy already, but it never hurts to have some handy, especially if you have updates.

- **Some notes on the company** — You will probably have a few minutes to review your thoughts, so jot down the key points neatly on a piece of paper and stick it in your folder.

Try to take only the bare minimum into the interview room. Leave your briefcase in the hall cupboard of the firm or recruiting centre; women typically bring their handbag to the interview.

Behaviour

There are some time-tested best practices for conducting oneself in a stressful environment like a consulting interview.

- **Firm handshake** — It isn't that the firm handshake necessarily enhances one's impression of another; it's that a weak handshake usually causes a negative impression. Don't try to crack your interviewer's knuckles or anything, just make sure you have a nice and solid grip. Wipe those sweaty palms on a handkerchief before you go in.

- **Maintain eye contact** — Try not to look down as you speak, and, except for when you need to write or glance at your notes, keep your head high and speak to the interviewer. Think of the interview as a conversation, not a test.

- **Speak slowly** — When people are nervous, they tend to speak faster. The result is that your interviewer will think you are less articulate than you really are and worry about your cool under pressure. Try to be aware of your overall tempo. If you finding yourself rushing, just relax, take a deep breath, and slow down. Take ten seconds if you need to, or sip some water to stall. Here's another slowdown tactic: when you need to pause, instead of using "um," say the word "now," as in "now…looking at the company's costs…" You'll find this works as a natural break in the action without losing the overall flow.

- **Keep out the distractions** — Try to avoid little movements and gestures that divert the interviewer's attention from the content of the interview. Examples include constantly brushing your hair out of your eyes, checking a clock or your watch, fidgeting, itching, or playing with your pen. We all do these things; in the interview context, they reflect insecurity. When you practice your interviews with others, ask for their feedback on the little distractions. You can also set yourself up for success by tying your hair back and keeping your watch at home.

- **Be good-natured and energetic.** Smile. Don't slump. Don't touch your face. Speak passionately about the things that matter to you and stay optimistic. If you get a bizarre question, laugh it off and do your best. After all, it's just an interview!

- **Ask for feedback.** After your interview, if you think you've had good rapport with your interviewer, ask for a 10-second summary of your strengths and weaknesses. Consultants must be willing to ask for, and accept feedback. Being proactive will work in your favour. At the very least, it will help you with future interviews. When possible, ask for a business card. If you get one, it implies that the interviewer is happy to have you contact him.

Pre-Interview Check List

It's the morning of your interview. You have done all your reading, you have researched the company, practiced your case study skills, practised talking through your CV, ironed a shirt and put on the suit you picked up from the dry cleaners yesterday ...and are ready to go. Or are you?

Check through the list below to see if you have got everything

- Have a good look in the mirror and check that the tie sits right, the shoelaces are tied and there are no ugly stains on the shirt

- Write down the address of your interview (make sure you know how to get there as well!)

- Remember the name of the person to ask for and make sure you know how to pronounce the name

  - Pen, pencil (take two, just in case)
  - Paper / Pad
  - A copy of your resume, just in case

Can you tick all the points off? Then you are ready to go! Good luck!

Visit **Vault Europe's Consulting Career Channel** at **www.Vault.com/Europe** for insider firm profiles, employee surveys of consultants in Europe, job listings, expert consulting career advice, insider salary information and more.

VAULT CAREER LIBRARY 91

Post-Interview: Accepting, Negotiating, Declining

CHAPTER 6

After the Interview

Whew! Wait until you walk out of the firm's lift bank or your university's career centre; then you can at last take a deep breath, relax, and enjoy the rest of the day. Then, start thinking about the next steps in the interview process.

Confirm next steps

If you just finished an interview round on campus, you probably already know the next steps (the firm's recruiter will call you Thursday, you will get an e-mail with the results, etc.). If you interviewed outside of the university's official recruiting cycles, or perhaps if you just finished final round interviews at the firm's city office, you will want to get some expectation of when you will hear the results. The easiest thing to do is to remember to ask the recruiting manager (likely not one of your interviewers) on the way out the door. If you forget, you can simply send an e-mail or give the recruiting contact a call the next day to confirm.

Thank your interviewers

Good form includes sending a thank-you note to your interviewers. This can be a very short message that thanks the interviewer for his or her time, reminds the person of one or two key items that you discussed, and reiterates why you are sincerely interested in the firm. Mention a couple of discussion points from the interview, because the interviewers speak to so many candidates that they will appreciate the teasers you send to refresh their memory (and will likely make you stand out in their minds).

A letter or thank-you note used to be the best way, but these days, an e-mail to the interviewer works fine. Send the thank-you note no later than the day after the interview.

Waiting for an offer

Perhaps the most stressful time of the entire process is after all the interviews, waiting to see if you got the job or not. Realise that at this point you've done all you can, and the decision is now fully out of your hands. You might as well enjoy the fact that you don't have to worry about this firm for a little while.

Visit **Vault Europe's Consulting Career Channel** at **www.Vault.com/Europe** for insider firm profiles, employee surveys of consultants in Europe, job listings, expert consulting career advice, insider salary information and more.

VAULT CAREER LIBRARY 93

So what do you do when the agreed-upon day of reckoning comes, and there's no phone call? This will happen from time to time. Be patient. Wait a day, then call your recruiting contact to find out where you stand. A call works better than an e-mail, because it is more personal and reminds the firm that you are waiting on pins and needles.

If you are going through on-campus recruiting and do not receive the answer within three to five business days of the date you were given for the firm's reply deadline, notify your career services office. The career office acts as your agent and enforces guidelines for the firms.

Accepting an Offer

One of the firm's partners has called to extend you an offer to join the firm. In a few days, you will formally receive the offer in writing. Congratulations! This is exactly what you've been working towards, and now you've got it.

If you've read the offer letter word by word and you are pleased with the package, you have the delightful job of informing the firm that you wish to accept the offer. Telling the firm "yes" is the fun and easy part. There are three steps. Leave a phone message with the recruiting manager, so they know to expect your paperwork in the mail. Sign and photocopy all of the documents. Send in the paperwork. That's it!

We recommend that you don't turn down other offers until you have formally accepted another. Also, do not consider a verbal offer a real offer-wait until you get it in writing. If you've negotiated any additional points in your offer letter, be sure that you've captured them in an e-mail at the very least. Getting items in writing on the firm's letterhead is better. You may need to refer to them later.

Visit **Vault Europe's Consulting Career Channel** at **www.Vault.com/Europe** for insider firm profiles, employee surveys of consultants in Europe, job listings, expert consulting career advice, insider salary information and more.

VAULT CAREER LIBRARY 95

Negotiating an Offer

Many candidates wish to negotiate the terms of their offer. Be warned that the extent to which you can negotiate the terms of your offer depends highly on the balance of power in the job market. In the late 1990s, the job market was an employee's market: Corporate growth was all the rage and companies would add extra benefits like a few thousand more dollars on the signing bonus or an extra week of holiday, in order to get employees in the door. In the early years of the current decade, it was a recruiter's market: New jobs were few and far between, and the lucky candidates with job offers were being given lower compensation and fewer benefits, with little room for negotiation.

Now, things have evened out — negotiation is easier but there are no lavish giveaways. That said, there are some time-tested best practices for negotiating consulting offers. No matter how the economy's doing, it is always worth a try. Just make sure you're pleasant and businesslike.

Office location

Changing locations after the offer is given is tough. Unless you have a compelling reason for the switch, you may find it difficult to change offices. Your chances are better if you're trying to switch from a more desirable office to an understaffed office.

Whatever the reason, first try explaining the reason for your office change to your recruiting manager and ask that person to look into the switch. They will either tell you no off the bat or look into the transfer. If the person agrees to look into the matter, make sure you both commit to a later date to follow up. Certain offices of some consultancies are designed as 'staffing offices,' allowing the smaller local offices to draw upon their resources. Make sure you are aware where the majority of projects of the office take place in order to avoid misunderstandings.

What if your request is turned down? Don't quit there. See if you can find someone in the target office to vouch for the office transfer — the higher up (partner or senior manager), the better. When you have found the person, explain your situation, describe why you really want to be a part of that person's office community and ask if there's anything he or she can do. Offer to visit the office and meet with the consultants there in person. (If they agree to this, your trip will be worth the money.) This is obviously a different angle to pursue, but it's worth a shot.

Start date

Some firm's will consider deferring your entry for a period of time. Often this has to be a full year because their training programmes are only run once. However, it is essential to ask early and to have a good reason for doing so. You might not choose to request deferral until you have an offer, but it is worth asking a junior member of staff at a presentation if they know what the policy is should you consider it. If the firm advertises that you can defer your entry, then they will expect you to mention this sooner rather than later. But be warned, in the past if the economy turned down in the year of deferral, some candidates found their offers withdrawn with little or no compensation. If you are particularly keen to start addressing your student loans, you can volunteer to start earlier, which might also be possible depending on how busy the company is and their training and induction schedules and policies   If you don't ask, you don't get!

Salary and bonus

Getting more money is always tough, especially in a recruiter's market, so don't expect to be able to improve your compensation package. (Just be glad you have one!) The best point of leverage would be to have another job offer in hand that offers more money. You can tell your firm contacts, "I really like your firm best; however, I have to admit that this competing offer is compelling because the salary is £5,000 higher. I'm ready to sign with you if we can make my numbers better. What can you do to improve my compensation package?" If you are an MBA or a lateral hire, you might have another point of negotiation if your previous salary was higher, because then you might be able to convince the employer that you are being undervalued.   Do not invent a fake job offer for negotiating leverage.

Starting position

An MBA with prior consulting experience or lateral hire might be given a first-year associate offer. If you are one of these people, and you feel like you are starting at a lower level than you should be, ask for a shorter initial review cycle, such as after six months instead of one year. This gives you a chance to prove your worth. If you can successfully negotiate for a shorter review period, don't forget to get it in writing; it would be easy for the firm to let this slip through the cracks.

Visit **Vault Europe's Consulting Career Channel** at **www.Vault.com/Europe** for insider firm profiles, employee surveys of consultants in Europe, job listings, expert consulting career advice, insider salary information and more.

VAULT CAREER LIBRARY 97

Leave

If you don't like the leave package and the firm won't grant you any more holidays, ask about the firm's unpaid leave policy. If the firm doesn't have one, get written confirmation (e-mail is fine) that you would be able to take extra days of unpaid holiday. There is no reason why a firm shouldn't be willing to not pay you for a few days a year.

Offer response deadline

Your offer letter will usually have a date listed, stating when you should let HR know you're either coming on board or not. Don't forget to ask for a deadline extension if you need it — surprisingly, this often turns out to be negotiable. It's a very common thing to get a little more time to make a decision, so don't feel weird about asking for it.

Turning Down an Offer

You may be one of those lucky people with more than one consulting offer, which means that you will have to turn down one or more of them. The goal is to turn down the offer in such a way that you stand the best chance of preserving your relationship with the firm.

A prime example of the importance of relationship management involves a 2001 graduate of a prestigious MBA programme named Edward. Edward was deciding between two equally compelling job offers from top consultancies, Firm 1 and Firm 2. Edward chose Firm 1 over Firm 2, based on a higher pay package (a difference of £15,000) and a location that would keep him closer to his wife. When Edward conveyed his decline of the offer to Firm 2, he stressed the fact that he really wanted to work at Firm 2 (which was entirely true), that the location was the deciding factor, and that he really wanted to make the relationship with Firm 2 work. Firm 2 understood, and told him that if he could indeed get the location to work out, Edward would be always welcome to join Firm 2 if it had a job for him.

As luck (bad luck, in this case) would have it, Firm 1 soon delayed Edward's start date indefinitely. Edward immediately called up Firm 2, explained the situation, and offered to move to a different location away from his wife. Firm 2 said it was not in a strong enough economic position to re-extend the offer, but invited Edward to keep in touch. Once a month, Edward called his contacts at Firm 2 to remind them that he was still available. Each time, Firm 2 said it still was not in a position to hire him. Nine months later, Firm 2 called Edward, informed him that it was looking to staff up, and because of his efforts to stay in touch, was prepared to offer him a position with the firm. He accepted, and he and his wife moved to the city where Firm 2 was headquartered. He still works with Firm 2 to this day. Meanwhile, Firm 1 never offered Edward a start date.

This is a true story of outstanding relationship management, and in today's difficult employment environment we encourage you to manage all of your relationships this well. We suggest a few guidelines for declining an offer and preserving your relationship with that firm.

- **Comply with the deadlines** — Even if you must decline an offer, tell the firm of your decision by the appropriate deadline.

- **Call instead of e-mailing** — E-mail is still a relatively impersonal form of communication. Remember that you are communicating a rejection to someone else. A team of partners sat around a table, thought hard, and decided to bring you into their firm. You should follow up with a note or e-mail.

Visit **Vault Europe's Consulting Career Channel** at **www.Vault.com/Europe** for insider firm profiles, employee surveys of consultants in Europe, job listings, expert consulting career advice, insider salary information and more.

VAULT CAREER LIBRARY 99

- **Be polite** — Be straightforward and even mildly apologetic when you break the news. Express your gratitude for the offer.

- **Try to frame your reason as external** — The firm will likely ask you for a reason why you choose not to work with them. Present the reason that seems the least personal. Suppose, for example, that you choose ABC over XYZ was for two reasons — you found XYZ's people to be nice but slightly aloof, and because XYZ's offer was for Birmingham and ABC's offer was for Leeds, where your parents live. You might offer the following as a reason for not choosing XYZ: "I really wanted to work at XYZ, but in the end I needed to be closer to my family in Leeds. I hope to make the relationship with XYZ work in the future." This approach will help preserve your relationship with XYZ.

Again, before you turn down any offers in favour of another, wait until you have accepted the other offer and received confirmation.

What to Do When Things Don't Work Out

Dealing with rejection (and overcoming it)

If you don't get an offer after the interview, don't take it personally. Remember that literally thousands of people must have applied for the job you did, and most of them didn't even get interviews.

First, make sure that you get feedback on your interview. Seek to understand what you did well and what areas you can improve. Most firms will volunteer this information. If you didn't receive feedback, ask for it.

You also want to find out when you might apply again. Do you need to wait until the next autumn? Or, if you work a different job in the meantime, could you get hired off-cycle as a lateral hire? Find out when to get in touch (if you are still interested in working with the firm) and whom to contact.

If it sounds like you were close to an offer, and you can identify the decision makers, you may want to make the following suggestions to still get your foot in the door.

- Project employment — Acknowledge that the firm has doubts about you. State that you are committed to the firm. Suggest that you work with the firm on one project only. Point out that this gives the firm help on projects, yet binds them in no way. You can further sweeten the deal for the firm by confirming that you wouldn't need benefits as a contractor.

- Work for free — This is the way to get experience under your belt if you have no other offers. Simply offer your services without pay on a per-project basis. Part-time work may also be effective.

- Backup materials — What do they have doubts about? If it's your writing ability, send them a sample. If it's brains, e-mail some backup results or a letter of reference. Perhaps you can change their perception of you.

Obviously, it is very difficult to overcome a denial of an offer, but we know folks for whom these strategies have worked. It may work for you.

Dealing with rescinded offers

An unfortunate consequence of the weak economy in the early 2000s was that many consulting firms resorted to rescinding or delaying job offers they'd given. This was

Visit **Vault Europe's Consulting Career Channel** at **www.Vault.com/Europe** for insider firm profiles, employee surveys of consultants in Europe, job listings, expert consulting career advice, insider salary information and more.

VAULT CAREER LIBRARY 101

obviously very disruptive to those prospective consultants unfortunate enough to have their job offers evaporate or recede into the hazy future.

- **If a firm rescinds its offer to you, try to understand what this means**. Will they never honour the offer? Have they rescinded all offers? What is the procedure for getting taken on, if any? Would you get any special consideration in the next go-around, given how unfairly you have been treated and how you turned down other offers in favour of the promises made by their firm? In compensation for lost income at the rescinding firms and the missed income from offers you turned down, what severance package will you get? Understand what the true impact is on you and what benefits you might get.

- **Attempt to negotiate a delayed start date instead of a rescinded offer.** A delayed start would mean that when the economy picks up and the firm can make good on its offers, you will be hired first because you've already passed the screening process. In other words, you are saving them money.

- **If you can't get a delayed start date, push for a severance package.** Firms should offer you something.

- **Rescinded offers are taboo on campus.** Several business schools (such as Harvard and Wharton) will put firms on probation for a set period of time should they rescind offers. If you're on campus, tell your career services centre so they can take appropriate actions.

- **Now is the time to tap into your network for other opportunities.** If you turned down other offers, start with those firms, as well as any firms you interviewed with but didn't get offers from. Offer options in the vein of those we listed in the previous section.

- **In all likelihood, you are stuck with restarting the recruiting cycle.** However, be cheered by the fact that you are no doubt in good company with the others in the same boat.

You might feel like your world is collapsing in on you if your offer is rescinded. Take a deep breath. Understand what it means, tap into your network, and remember that things will work out.

Dealing with delayed offers

Difficult economic climates facilitated the creation of the delayed start date, also known as a deferral. A deferral is a rather creative way for HR departments to manage their employment flow.

Firms simply inform their new recruits that they will have to delay their start date, and often offer them the chance to walk away or wait for the start date to kick in. In some cases, firms have offered cash to continue waiting; in others, firms have offered cash equivalents (like the keeping of a signing bonus) for new recruits to walk away and exit the firm's job pipeline. This works out well from the firm's standpoint — they avoid rescinding offers, and don't have to pay salaries. In effect, they have purchased an option on future employees.

As a deferred new hire, what can you do? You can attempt to accelerate your recruiting process. This is obviously difficult, but there are things you can try. Call up the partner who hired you or any other senior person you know, explain your situation (they might not even know about it) and ask if you could work on a per-project or part-time basis with them. Many firms have an infrastructure to bring on cheap labour like outside consultants — why not you, since you've been pre-screened? If your contact doesn't require your help, push to see if he or she will circulate your CV to colleagues. If you can somehow get into the system, you might be able to get hired more quickly. Confirm who your official firm contact is, and stay on that person's radar. Call them up monthly to get an update, even if there's nothing to report. Strive to be first in that person's mind should an interim opportunity arise.

If you have no other job options, you should stay in the pipeline, because eventually (though who knows when) you will have a job at that company. There is absolutely no point in stepping out of the pipeline — why destroy a future option for yourself.

At the same time, continue your job search. The problem with being deferred is that you feel like you're in limbo. This could prevent you from entering a full-fledged job search. The fact is, if you've been deferred, you currently have no job. Please don't fall into the trap of thinking that you do.

Go to your network of job contacts (again, anywhere you have an "in," especially offers you've turned down and firms where you got an interview) and start the cycle again.

In the interim, you will have some time to yourself. Keep your brain sharp by studying and reading. See if you can help out your favourite professors from university or business school with research or their own consulting positions.

Finally, don't forget to stay in touch with your friends and family — use this opportunity to make sure your emotional "bank account" is full.

Visit **Vault Europe's Consulting Career Channel** at www.Vault.com/Europe for insider firm profiles, employee surveys of consultants in Europe, job listings, expert consulting career advice, insider salary information and more.

VAULT CAREER LIBRARY **103**

CAREER GUIDE

ON THE JOB

CONSULTING

Project Types and the Project Life Cycle

CHAPTER 7

Types of Consulting Projects

Consultants are exposed to a wide range of project types throughout their careers. Nevertheless, projects can be loosely grouped into a number of broad categories.

Strategy projects

On strategy engagements, a client asks a consultancy to review and evaluate its overall strategic direction. This typically happens after a leadership change or disappointing financial results, though pressure from the board of directors sometimes initiates the engagement. The consultants examine whether their client is competing in attractive market sectors or is vulnerable to fundamental market shocks, or both. The team might recommend acquisitions or divestments, shifts in emphasis on reinvestment in the business, or a methodology for achieving higher shareholder returns.

Strategy projects often lead to additional types of work for consulting firms. Do an outstanding job for your client, and you will probably gain enough of their confidence to implement the strategy as well. If the client is impressed with the consulting firm's process and results, it will seek its counsel on an ongoing basis.

Sales/marketing/distribution projects

Consultants are increasingly asked to assess marketing and distribution strategy, particularly as technology's impact on distribution grows. Teams are frequently asked to recommend the most preferable distribution channel or to assess if distribution via parallel channels is viable. They are also asked to propose more effective marketing strategies or to evaluate how the sales force functions within the client company.

Regardless of what you end up recommending, chances are that many people will be affected: job descriptions change because employees need to learn new functions, technologies, and/or processes, and vendor and customer relationships are also at risk of being affected. Just remember to take all these potential impacts into consideration when presenting your final recommendations. You want to ensure that everyone touched by the proposed changes willingly accepts and looks forward to them. Any resistance poses a threat to your project's overall success.

Visit **Vault Europe's Consulting Career Channel** at **www.Vault.com/Europe** for insider firm profiles, employee surveys of consultants in Europe, job listings, expert consulting career advice, insider salary information and more.

V/\ULT CAREER LIBRARY **107**

Reorganisation projects

As more companies expand globally and make more acquisitions, their traditional organisation structure sometimes becomes unwieldy. Consultants often advise their clients on how to become optimal organisations during these times — considering centralisation vs. decentralisation, product vs. geography, line vs. matrix. Because these projects often involve reallocation of power or territory, they can be political minefields. People get laid off or moved into different job descriptions. Entire departments are moved, cut, or created. New systems are implemented. New decision-making policies are developed. Employees must learn new ways to approach their daily functions. That's why the consultants are called in: they represent a neutral party.

While employees are the most affected in a reorganisation, consultants often forget to consider the people first. But you should never forget the people affected; one day, they might become future clients, bosses or necessary contacts. Treat them well, and with sensitivity and compassion. They will remember you.

Cost-cutting/re-engineering projects

Consultants are also called in when companies need to self-prescribe a bitter pill and prefer that an outsider take the blame. Cost-cutting does not just mean the identification of job redundancies. A cost-cutting project looks at all areas of cost and answers:

• Can the company reduce raw materials costs?
• Is there excess inventory?
• Are marketing funds being spent effectively?
• Are central costs being duplicated in the divisions?

This type of engagement tends to be hands-on, requires a significant period of time at the client site, and can be very data-intensive. Its satisfaction lies in the concrete nature of its recommendations and the immediate impact of saving the client money. These projects typically follow on the heels of a strategic consulting engagement.

Like reorganisation projects, these engagements also affect many people at very personal levels. Again, remember the people!

Project management/implementation

Clients find consultants useful as a third-party facilitator for large-scale projects involving a number of different departments within the company. Tasks might include the following:

- Facilitating a day-long brainstorming session identifying the key goals and drivers
- Creating a three month project implementation and testing plan
- Running daily status meetings and conference calls attended by all parties involved in the project
- Acting as an intermediary between different parties and resolving disputes

In short, a consultant on this sort of project would be doing anything required to manage the project and drive its successful completion. While this line of work tends not to be the most intellectually stimulating for the consultant, it requires thorough organisation, superb facilitation skills, and the ability to work well with a variety of people at once. In addition, such projects offer a recurring revenue stream to consultancies, with fees on a retainer basis. They can be the projects most vital to a consulting firm's bottom line.

Market study and due diligence projetcs

Consultants offer market study and due diligence services in a variety of cases and to a variety of client types. Often the motivation behind these cases is to achieve an unbiased opinion of a developing market, and consultancies offer a their research and analysis capabilities for this purpose.

The market studies can take different shapes depending on the key interest and the final audience but can be categorised in the following three types

- Market studies to facilitate understanding of market drivers to clients unfamiliar with the industry
- Commercial due diligence as part of the set of documents required by banks during merger & acquisition transactions
- Market review for existing participants in the market normally as part of a strategic review or customer feedback review

All of the above will involve a SWOT approach (see Industry Buzzwords) to market analysis that will cover the main drivers and most important trends in the industry, but with strategic assessments and commercial due diligence, this will be more specifically related to the company in question.

Also, while market studies tend to be less time-critical, the due diligence work often runs to tight deadlines and high expectations, making the projects often very intensive in nature.

Being staffed on a commercial due diligence project has its advantages as well. While most consulting assignments have long-term rather than short term repercussions, you are likely to read about your due diligence case in the papers shortly after finishing it.

Visit **Vault Europe's Consulting Career Channel** at **www.Vault.com/Europe** for insider firm profiles, employee surveys of consultants in Europe, job listings, expert consulting career advice, insider salary information and more.

VAULT CAREER LIBRARY **109**

The Project Life Cycle

Pitching/Letter of Proposal

In comparison to investment banks, management consultants spend comparatively little time in a formal pitching process. Partners carry out the main pitch process. They either respond to the initial approach of current or potential clients, or they identify new or follow-up studies with past clients. Associates generally get involved in some initial non-billable work (research, mainly) to support the partners' conversations with the client.

To do more than support the initial conversations, do your part to land new clients and engagements. Research the industry for new studies your firm would want to publish. Approach past clients for organisational pulse checks. When at a client, keep your eyes and ears open for new opportunities. Tap your alumni network effectively — surf the online directory for alums that are senior managers in your target industries and get advice from partners in your firm on leveraging that point of contact. By taking these steps, you become more visible and might even receive a nice bonus, raise, or promotion for all your efforts.

The ultimate aim of the pitch process is the drafting of a Letter of Proposal, also called a Letter of Intent (LOP/LOI). The LOP lays out how and on what the consulting team will focus their efforts, and what results the client should expect. LOPs also detail consulting and client resources and expected length of the engagement. And they might or might not touch upon the sensitive topic of remuneration.

Although the letter itself might be a little dry and boring, try to get involved in the engagement at this early stage. First, it provides a good chance to get up to speed on the client and industry before the study starts in earnest. Second, you might mitigate a partner's optimistic estimates of the team's performance efficiency and make yourself a hero in the end.

Brainstorming/Hypothesis generation

With the LOP signed, the engagement starts. The first few days are normally spent in an intensive round of brainstorming involving the whole consulting team and sometimes client members. The team digs into the details, generates a spectrum of options to investigate, and narrows these down to a few hypotheses. This approach, used by most major consulting firms, limits the data gathering and analysis to prevent considering an overly broad range of data.

Brainstorming can be both the most exciting and the most frustrating stage of the project. On the one hand, a new consultant sees firsthand how more senior team members tackle the problem set before them. On the other hand, the team might not seem to be making much headway. Ideas are tossed about without any data backing them up. Sensitive egos get bruised because some ideas are rejected. But effective communication (which includes the underestimated power of listening well) during these sessions will guarantee you brainstorming success.

The final part of brainstorming takes each emerging hypothesis and determines how to prove or disprove it in the analysis stage. The team creates a course of action for each case by deciding:

- What data will be required?
- How will it be gathered?
- Who will take responsibility for each part of the analysis?
- How will results be presented?
- How will issues be determined and resolved?
- What information will carry the most weight?

Data gathering and analysis

The meat of the engagement is the data gathering and analysis phase. Although the hypothesis helps focus the task, data gathering can still be overwhelming. Many consultants fear "boiling the ocean" (see the Appendix for industry buzz words) at this stage — considering an impossibly large amount of data. Your initial port of call is your firm's in-house consulting library, and the second option is asking the client for pertinent information — both of which tend to result in large stacks of articles, brokers' and annual reports and other reference materials. You then identify experts or consultants from your firm, who hold similar but non-conflicting projects in their portfolios.

During this stage, you tap internal sources of information provided by the client, from systems and databases to extensive interviews with client personnel. Some studies require you to consult industry experts for their experience, while others necessitate more hands-on measures. Hands-on measures tend not to be so glamorous. Some real-life examples include sitting outside a competitor's factory to count in- and out-going trucks over several days and taking an inventory of an ice cream company's flavours from inside huge freezers.

However the data is collected, there will be plenty of it — but remember that none of the data will exactly prove or disprove your point. This is where a consultant's ingenuity comes to bear: re-cutting data, combining data sources and making judicious assumptions

Visit **Vault Europe's Consulting Career Channel** at www.Vault.com/Europe for insider firm profiles, employee surveys of consultants in Europe, job listings, expert consulting career advice, insider salary information and more.

V/\ULT   CAREER LIBRARY   **111**

to support or negate the hypothesis you are trying to test. (Just be sure your clients and your management sign off on your assumptions before proceeding!)

Pulling out conclusions and building the story

Developing a story is an evolving process throughout the project, and it starts at hypothesis generation. As a forcing mechanism, many consultants draft a flexible final presentation at this stage, based on their emerging hypotheses. This process is often called 'blank sliding' and helps consultants focus and plan their workstreams. The team integrates new analysis into the overall puzzle, notes the ripple effects, and revises the analysis to take the changes into account. By developing the storyboard first, the team must regularly helicopter to the top (that is, take a big-picture view) and ensure they answer the client's key questions directly. However, this method sometimes fails because of its rigidity, which is why consultants often use primary and secondary storyboards from the start. Other consulting firms like to start with one story and map out many endings to see which ones are most effective.

Presentation to client

How frequently and in what format the team updates the client varies widely, depending on the engagement. When the client is involved on a day-to-day basis, communication tends to be more frequent and informal. If most of the analysis takes place at the office, client updates might be scheduled on a biweekly or monthly basis. These updates are two-way and critical to the success of the project. During these sessions, the client communicates what its management wants or thinks.

This is also your opportunity to confirm the project's direction and success. "Scope creep" — when clients add additional tasks and expectations to a project — often delays timely success. You must understand how to manage your client's expectations throughout the project, but most especially at these status meetings. However, if your client insists, create an addendum to your LOP, get it signed and notify your management of these changes immediately.

Consultants present each finished phase of a project and their major findings to the board of directors. Formal presentations are posed as a landscape of exhibits, held together by a story line. The partner or director generally runs the meeting. A manager usually makes the presentation, though this job sometimes falls to an associate who had assumed ownership for part of the project. If the project has been run well, the clients will encounter no major surprises.

Tips for High Performance

CHAPTER 8

Troubleshooting

Introverts need not apply

Many consultants are fresh out of top universities, smooth operators eager to make their mark in the business world. They may lack industry knowledge or know little about the fundamentals of big business, but they know how to interact with people. No one gets a job offer in consulting without having a penchant for person-to-person interaction. Clients absolutely demand it and consulting firms consider it a prerequisite for the job.

Consulting firms actively screen candidates for the ability to establish professional relationships, handle pressure, and communicate effectively. Consulting interviews, apart from being tools to learn a candidate's background, are meant to test these skills and see how candidates will perform in front of clients. The whole experience is a simulation where the candidate plays the role of consultant, and the firm sits back and judges what it hears. Did you structure your thoughts? Were you comfortable answering complex questions? Were you convincing?

The most common mistake for would-be consultants is to concentrate so strongly on acing case questions that they forget to be engaging and personable with their interviewers. Clients want more than long, hyper-logical answers to every question. They also want to make small talk, trade stories and feel as if they are a valuable part of the conversation. Consulting interviewers are on the lookout for anyone who, despite being extremely intelligent, cannot communicate in a way that makes the client feel involved and appreciated. Those people will not get job offers.

Of course, clients are often twice as demanding and create far greater challenges than anything experienced in consulting interviews. Consulting training, therefore, is geared heavily toward preparing new recruits for an ever-demanding professional experience. Being smooth gets you in the door, but it's only a foundation for the advanced skills you will need down the road.

Keep your counsel

One of the first lessons new consultants must learn is the proper care and feeding of clients. It's not uncommon for new recruits to be overwhelmed and uncertain at first about how to deal with clients. Clients are often much older than new consultants. It's often unclear who's in charge of consulting projects, the consultant or the client. And it's easy to mistake a good working relationship for a stronger bond.

Experienced consultants, however, know how to play by the implicit client-consultant rules. They never forget, first and foremost, that a client is a client, not a buddy. This might seem obvious, but it's not unheard of for consultants to let down their guard during a friendly golf game or a client dinner. Tell your client that his boss is a moron, and even if you're right, you shouldn't be surprised to find yourself yanked unceremoniously from the engagement. And neither the client nor your employer will be happy with you. Respect your clients, but don't get too close.

Sell, don't study

For consulting managers and partners, the essence of consulting has little to do with locating a client's problems, identifying solutions or driving large-scale change. Consulting, at its fundamental core, is about completing the terms of relationship, making the client happy and getting a referral for more business. That is the primary focal point of consulting engagements: selling. Consulting executives know that all the brilliance in the world doesn't matter unless, at the end of the project, the client is happy. That means if you don't make the client happy, your manager will not be happy with you.

Some consultants have a hard time understanding this. Armed with their Fulbright scholarships, valedictorian plaques or reputations for solving difficult problems at the speed of light, some consultants have difficulty prioritising interpersonal relations over intellectual achievement. Of course, smarts and creative thinking are essential to the completion of the consultant's tasks. But — and this is a big but — if the project is completed through steamrolling client objections, scoffing at client ideas, and otherwise behaving in an arrogant, "I'm-24-and-run-the-company" manner, your client will still be unhappy.

Your client is not stupid

Many consulting engagements are held in the confines of large, corporate headquarters where organisational clarity is, in theory, supposed to exist. Upon arriving at a client site, consultants are often taken aback by the lack of process, frustrated by the poor communication between departments and shocked that no one seems to care. How the hell does this place make money? "I," thinks the new consultant, "could do a better job in two months than the leaders of this place could do in a lifetime."

This sort of arrogance is all too common in consultants. Overconfident consultants think that by observing the client for a while or by reading a brief company history, they will be able to identify and solve every single problem that exists. What they fail to realise is that people on the client team have been working in the company for years, sometimes decades. Their institutional knowledge can be extensive and extremely helpful, and their ability to manoeuvre through their company's culture can save consultants a lot of heartache. Scoff at your own risk. Clients often know more about their companies than you ever will, so rely on them for occasional help — or drown in your own ignorance. The more clients in different positions you can engage in your line of questioning, the more balanced your view will be.

Be careful in your attitude towards the client. Clients know when consultants do not approve of the job they are doing. And have some sensitivity. It's galling to have all your problems examined openly by strangers — and used as examples of faulty thinking.

Do you still think the client is stupid? Just remember that the client hired you, so how stupid can they be? Also recall that the client pays your salary. The client has the power to support, or not support, every single initiative consultants so brilliantly suggest. Anger the client and you may as well start writing the project's obituary.

Like it or not, the client is central to consulting projects. Consulting may have the allure of being a think-tank experience with no running commentary from outside observers, but that is only half true. The reality is that clients are involved in the process nearly every day, that factions within companies have power (and need to be neutralised) and that right answers, no matter how impressive, are worthless without client buy-in.

Nothing does more to stunt a consultant's learning than this type of attitude. In fact, it is nearly impossible to consult with any effectiveness if the client is stereotyped, underestimated or ignored. Clients hold the keys to mountains of useful information, and they either make this information available or they don't.

Consulting versus body-shopping

Consulting doesn't always involve wining and dining CEOs and offering high-level strategy advice to beleaguered corporations. Sometimes consultants are mere soldiers on

Visit **Vault Europe's Consulting Career Channel** at www.Vault.com/Europe for insider firm profiles, employee surveys of consultants in Europe, job listings, expert consulting career advice, insider salary information and more.

V\ULT CAREER LIBRARY **115**

the battleground of business, conducting training seminars, crunching numbers in nameless Excel spreadsheets, even making catering arrangements for conferences.

Consulting, traditionally speaking, centres around the client relationship, the exchange of ideas and advice, the large question-answer sessions that lead to corporate breakthroughs, long, raucous client dinners and real, progressive change. This is the dream offered by strategy shops like McKinsey, Bain, Mercer and the like. But much of what the average consultant actually does involves coding in a hastily-learned computer language, trying out PowerPoint skills to compile presentations, writing memos and other maintenance tasks that almost certainly could be done more cheaply by the client's employees. This is, for lack of a better word, called body-shopping.

Sometimes, consultants may begin an engagement as strategists and end as body shop workers. For many client teams, sticking to original project plans is a very difficult task. Clients often see consultants as a fresh source of labour. If consulting executives don't push back and enforce the original agreement, consultants may end up doing routine tasks. Body-shopping engagements often end badly, with both client and consultancy trying to figure out why the highly-skilled consultants ended up doing such routine work.

How To Survive Your First Team Assignment

You're a team

The first few weeks at a consulting firm are a crash course in teamwork, and job seekers often underestimate the extent to which collaboration determines a project's success. A common misperception is that consultants sit down with corporate vice presidents, tell them what to do, and watch the client's metamorphosis. The truth is that nothing gets accomplished without extensive discussion, countless status meetings and plenty of ad-hoc brainstorming sessions where everyone involved works feverishly to build a consensus.

Over the course of your career in consulting, you will be a member of many teams, often simultaneously. At a client site, for example, you may be working on an implementation team while also sitting down with a proposal team to generate new work. Additionally, you might be working on an "internal" team to develop new community service programmes for your own firm. In the course of your workday, you could interact with as many as six different teams, all with different objectives and time commitments. If you have an aversion to meetings, or if you envision a career defined by isolated thinking and long stretches of time without any human interaction, consulting probably isn't the right choice for you.

Close quarters, high pressure

Since you'll depend on your client for your office space, be prepared to work in non-lavish conditions. At one client site, your project team may have limited access to conference rooms and be forced to hold meetings in a cubicle. At another client site, your team may be sharing a single office with one small window and very little space. Part of your job will be to learn to be productive with frequent interruptions. More often than not, you will share limited technical resources such as printers, copiers, fax machines and LAN lines.

It all comes with the nature of the job. Consultants are high-priced migrant workers; they must know how to pack their bags, move to another location and set up shop, all in the blink of an eye and with little choice in the matter. But whether they are working in a crowded office space, a hotel suite late at night, or on a flight home, good consultants develop a set of behaviours that makes their jobs much easier.

Some coping tips:

- Take personal calls on your mobile phone, away from the project team.
- If you are frustrated with a software program, take a walk and come back with a positive outlook.
- Speak only when necessary in order to keep the noise down in the project room.
- Keep your work space uncluttered.

These simple rules can improve a project's efficiency and the quality of life for your fellow consultants.

Know the objectives

Most productive meetings address a set of objectives, assign individual tasks to support the objectives, and set timelines for completion. While this process is fairly routine in a consultant's workweek, the abundance of meetings can have a deadening effect; consultants can spend more time thinking about their mountain of pending work than the actual meeting they are attending.

Walking away from a meeting with only a vague idea of its objectives can lead to a variety of problems, not the least of which is having to meet all over again. Consulting firms operate on tight schedules. Project managers generally do not tolerate having to repeat critical directives, because they are pressed for time and need each component of the team to produce solid results.

Once a meeting is brought to a close, you should walk away with a notepad filled with key points from the discussion and a specific list of your own "to do" items. If you are unclear

Visit **Vault Europe's Consulting Career Channel** at **www.Vault.com/Europe** for insider firm profiles, employee surveys of consultants in Europe, job listings, expert consulting career advice, insider salary information and more.

VAULT CAREER LIBRARY 117

about a certain portion of the meeting, you should raise the issue immediately, rather than spend your time guessing how to proceed. For each and every meeting, no matter how irrelevant it seems, your attention to detail can make or break your performance on the project team. Don't expect anyone to keep you awake. Fellow consultants are bogged down with their own assignments, and even though they may engage you in small talk, the expectation is that you will deliver results — on time and consistent with the original objectives.

Whatever it takes

If consulting firms seem demanding when trying to meet deadlines, the clients can be downright unforgiving. At the start of every project, the thought of missing deadlines simply does not occur to consultants, nor does the prospect of creating anything but high-quality deliverables. The ugly reality is that executives do not always budget enough time or allot enough resources to meet the client's expectations. The result is that consultants must bring a "whatever it takes" attitude to work every day.

If a 60-hour workweek doesn't appear to be enough to get your required work done, then you add on more hours. If a printer breaks down on the night before a big presentation, then you have to find one, even if it means a late night drive to KallKwik. Sometimes, during the end of projects, you will squeeze massive amounts of work into small timeframes, and you may have to pull an all-nighter or two. These things happen in consulting, and consulting firms expect that you will take it all in stride. You do have some latitude with regard to personal time, but when important deadlines approach, getting out of an assignment is nearly impossible.

The good news is that never-say-die attitudes are contagious, and the longer you work in a consulting firm, the more you begin to appreciate spending time with people who value results so highly. People who leave the consulting profession are often disappointed to learn that their new company employs a more laissez-faire approach to everything it does. The consulting industry's sharp attention to deadlines is both its curse and its strength. Consultants initially bemoan the fact that their job is so demanding, but they often grow to love that very facet of it, and in some cases see it as justification for never switching careers.

Communicating with your team

Sometimes your team will go into head-down mode, where people are working independently on PowerPoint slides or financial models. As a new consultant, you want to take responsibility for updating your team leaders frequently on where you are with your work. Certainly, they will want to always have a best estimate of their project status. But this will help you, too, because the team leader has experience that you don't, and he or she will likely have some useful suggestions. Once a day is probably fine for an update.

When you are away from your team (say, on a Friday, when all team members are usually in their home office), use voice mail for updates and questions. Most consulting firms communicate as a voice mail culture, meaning that the equivalent to calling a person directly is to leave a voice mail. The recipient can simply hit the "reply" command to respond. Use voice mail for issues of medium urgency, and use e-mail when you can wait 24 hours or more for a response. By the same token, try to reply to each voice mail within two hours or so of its delivery.

Make sure your e-mail doesn't pile up, especially for your project work. To get yourself started on the right foot, play a little game with yourself: give yourself no more than 24 hours to respond to every work e-mail.

Ask lots of questions

Did one of your junior high teachers waggle his finger at your and claim, "The only stupid question is the one that's never asked?" Remember, you are a new consultant and you are not expected to know anything. If you are fresh out of university, you are not expected to know what a discount rate or DCF is. At MBA or lateral hire levels, you may have never seen a decision tree before. If you feel at all self-conscious about asking silly questions, you'd better stop it right now. Ask away! Internally, consulting is entirely about mentorship and grooming new consultants, and Q&A is the only way to learn.

At the beginning of your first few projects, take a minute during the kick-off meeting to remind your team members that you are still new to the firm, and you would like to set the expectation that you will be asking the team members lots of questions. This is a really good step to take because (1) It shows that you are proactive about learning and doing a great job and (2) Your more senior team members will be prepared to help you and not be surprised or frustrated when you come to them for help.

One great way to make sure you ask and answer your questions is to keep a question journal. Devote a couple of pages in your notebook to this task. When something comes up, write it down, whether it's about your firm's methodology, an industry term or how to find the online time tracking system. Once a day, flip through the questions and figure out which ones make sense to ask. Don't forget to jot the answer down next to the question when you're done.

It also helps to have a "buddy" in the firm who can be your go-to resource for mundane things like voice mail or expense guidelines. Many firms will actually assign you a buddy for this reason. If you are not assigned one, figure out who you feel most comfortable

Visit **Vault Europe's Consulting Career Channel** at **www.Vault.com/Europe** for insider firm profiles, employee surveys of consultants in Europe, job listings, expert consulting career advice, insider salary information and more.

VAULT CAREER LIBRARY 119

talking with and ask that person directly if he or she wouldn't mind being your resource for all things mundane. Again, the point of this isn't to get permission, but to set the expectation with the person that you will be coming to them for help.

Getting Staffed

Now that you have a consulting job, guess what? Your job search, in essence, begins all over again. That's because your first few assignments can be critical to your future at your firm. One frequent danger is pigeonholing. (The danger of this tends to be greater at larger consulting firms.) Complete a computer-based training module about Visual Basic, go on a few successful Visual Basic training assignments and voila! — you're a Visual Basic expert and will be staffed primarily, if not exclusively, on Visual Basic assignments. This is fine if you're got a desire to specialise, and even better if you happen to become an "expert" in an area where assignments are diverse and plentiful.

However, there can be drawbacks to such an approach. You might grow to loathe Visual Basic. You might be routinely staffed on assignments where travel is unavoidable. Visual Basic might be the furthest thing from your career goal.

Ask yourself a few questions. Where do you want to work? Do you want to travel? Do you want to work with a particular client? (Many consulting firms have bread-and-butter clients with whom they routinely work.) Do you want to stay with this firm for a few years, or for a career?

If you're not in an area you like — or worse, if you're not getting staffed at all — you have a few options. Do your best to receive training in an area that interests you. Ask those a level above you, as well as your mentor (whether informal or assigned by your firm) if they are aware of any current or upcoming projects in your preferred area. Some consulting companies have internal intranets; don't be shy about using yours to locate projects that interest you and the appropriate contacts.

You may or may not have a representative in human resources who staffs you. Make sure you meet your HR rep and communicate your preferences to him or her regularly. But be warned: while some HR reps are looking out for your best interests, many are simply trying to staff warm bodies.

If you're new to the organisation and know no one, you may not have any options. You may need to take whatever is given to you, be a team player and do the best job you can. If it's not your first choice, in a diplomatic way, make sure your HR rep knows that — to be able to better fit you to your next role. Then use that project to become known as a person who has a great attitude, can do anything, and is someone people want to work with.

Even if you despise your project, build relationships with project managers on every project you are staffed on. They are the front lines to the staffing opportunities; they decide who they want to be on their team. Those managers will also support you for promotion and help you navigate the company. Soon, you will be staffed directly on projects by your contacts.

Better Billing

By Hannah Im

Billing is an essential part of being a consultant. It's easy to fall into sloppy or even unethical billing; make sure this doesn't happen to you.

The honour policy

As consultants, it's very easy to take advantage of our accounting departments, especially in large firms where almost every consultant travels most of the time. Expenses add up quickly, and most accounting departments only spot check expense reports. We are supposed to submit our reports to our managers for their sign-off, so the accounting staff can focus on processing, rather than on reviewing each report. But when everyone is travelling and working long hours, the review policy can be somewhat lax.

Most of our managers expect us to abide by the unwritten honour policy. However, I've heard of many instances when this policy is abused. It is especially easy to abuse the policy when consultants receive per diems, instead of having to submit hard copy receipts for exact amount reimbursement. Consultants may exaggerate the cost of dinners, report a higher tip than they paid for their taxi rides, and charge through expenses under false scenarios. For example, some consultants double their receipts by going out for meals in large groups and allowing the one who paid to expense it, then expensing a portion for themselves too.

Then there are the expenses that just make no sense. I know of one firm that allows partners to expense their babies' nappies but frowns on directors who try to do the same. In another instance, consultants have "treated" their clients to topless clubs or pub crawls. The consultants charge through the expense as "client entertainment" or "project development" (or some such equivalent), though the client is ultimately billed for it anyway. Of course the clients see only the lump sum on their bills and usually refrain from asking to see the expense

Visit **Vault Europe's Consulting Career Channel** at **www.Vault.com/Europe** for insider firm profiles, employee surveys of consultants in Europe, job listings, expert consulting career advice, insider salary information and more.

VAULT CAREER LIBRARY 121

reports. But imagine the consequences if a client ever found out the actual expense.

Stealing from yourself

Expense reporting ethics are very important to the health of the firm. All financial concerns, be they incoming or outgoing, impact the firm's bottom line. This, in turn, affects consultants' bonuses. Also, if unethical behaviour is caught, it can debilitate a client relationship, not to mention result in an employee's termination. Additionally, imagine your spouse's reaction when you tell her you got fired for something as petty as lying about your expenses. Or try explaining it to a future employer.

You probably will not lose your job if you are ever caught. The more likely scenario is that management would have a conversation with you to make sure you understand the policy.

You will probably only lose your job if you take advantage of the system too frequently or get caught with unacceptably large sums. Be warned that the firm holds the right to take legal action against you, in addition to firing you.

By and large, consulting firms are very proud of their code of ethics. Our business is built on trust between the firm and its clients. Breach of expense reporting ethics is breaching the clients' trust. Put in more basic terms, cheating on expenses is no different than stealing. To make it worse, it is not stealing from an employer, but from your own pocket. The firm's revenues are put toward business continuity and your salary. To steal from the company is to steal from your future with the company and from the salary you would have received anyway. Moreover, dishonesty about your expenses is unfair to those who choose to be honest. So not only do you steal from your future with the company and your salary, you also steal from that of your colleagues.

Think twice

Sure, everyone does it once or twice. I admit to taking a taxi on the firm when I worked fewer hours than the policy states, only because I was too tired to take the train. I also admit to fabricating amounts when I lost the receipt and failed to remember the exact amount. I did so knowing that neither the firm nor the client was going to care about a difference of £20. And I did not allow it to become a habit. In total, I probably owe all my employers less than £300 over my entire career. I would not be surprised if others, including top-level management, owe similar amounts, if not more.

A few hundred dollars here and there, multiplied by hundreds of thousands of consultants adds up to impressive sums. That money could have been spent on training or better laptops or other resources that would help to improve your job performance. So next time you submit a report, think twice about how you write the report. Scrutinise your motives and the potential short-term and long-term consequences. If nothing else, by reporting your expenses accurately and honestly, at least you never have to wait for the reimbursement check, wondering if anyone will catch you in a stupid lie.

Hannah Im has been a consultant throughout her career. She specialises in business operations, specifically process improvement/reengineering and risk management. She has served as a consulting career expert for the Vault Consulting Career Channel at http://consulting.vault.com.

On the Beach

By the time you've worked in consulting for a few months, you'll be very familiar with the expression "on the beach." This simply means that you are not staffed on a client-billable project. The more consultants a firm has on the beach, the lower the firm's utilisation rate. In times when clients spend more on consultants, utilisation rates can be in the 90 percent range; in economic downturns, the industry's average firm utilisation rate can be as low as 50 percent.

Being on the beach is a mixed blessing for consultants. On the plus side, it means you are not travelling, for once, and you can come into the office at 9 a.m. and leave at 5 p.m. On the negative side, it means that you are not gaining any project experience, and the less project experience you have, the less development as a consultant you get, the less likelihood you have of being staffed and the higher chance you face of being let go by your firm. So while being on the beach for a little while is a good thing; too much beach time is something you want to avoid.

That said, there are some productive ways you can spend your beach time.

Play catch up

First, take some time to regroup. Take care of your expenses and time tracking. Clean your desk. Take care of that health insurance paperwork with your HR folks. Answer those nagging emails from a month ago. Everyone needs downtime for such things, and everyone you work with will understand that you deserve it.

Visit **Vault Europe's Consulting Career Channel** at **www.Vault.com/Europe** for insider firm profiles, employee surveys of consultants in Europe, job listings, expert consulting career advice, insider salary information and more.

VAULT CAREER LIBRARY 123

Don't feel bad about squeezing in a little personal time over a couple of days for errands. This is a good chance to get back to the dentist or do that physical you've been meaning to get out of the way. Also, you can finally have lunch with your university roommate. Don't go overboard with the personal stuff — just realise that this is a good time to fit a few things in.

Network for new projects

Revisit the mental process you went through the last time you were staffed. What did you get out of your last project? What are your current project goals? What industries would you be interested to work in next? What skills would you like to develop? Be sure to jot these down and keep them on the tip of your tongue, for you will need to start communicating these topics to others.

If you have someone assigned to staff you, let that person know you're available. You will need to start networking for a new project right away. Target a few partners and senior managers and leave them voice mails, letting them know that you are checking in and looking for a new project. If you're in the office, pop by a few desks and see if the partners you know are close to a selling a new piece of work, and let them know you're available. Remember that your contacts (partners and senior managers) are busy, so you will need to keep following up with them to see if new opportunities have materialised.

Marketing work

When firms aren't working on consulting engagements, they are working on acquiring them. You can guarantee that the partners selling work will always want help doing so. Such help will usually be in the form of research. You might write up an industry overview and do a competitive assessment. You might create a deck of slides on a potential client and come up with possible issues they are facing that might require the help of a consultancy. Or you might be put to work on a draft of the actual proposal.

Be sure to ask your contacts above if they need help on sales and marketing and offer your assistance. While they may not always have a live project available for you, they very likely could use your help elsewhere. If you help a partner sell work, he or she will already know that you are familiar with the client and would be likely to staff you on the project.

Internal studies

Many consulting firms put out white papers and articles. Many efforts are the pet projects of just a few people, so opportunities to work on them are few and far between, but sometimes the writers need extra help with research and editing. Find out who manages these efforts from your mentors in the firm. Call up those contacts and ask how you can help. You will probably have some chasing around to do, so keep at it. With luck, you might find yourself working on the next Harvard Business Review article. Some larger consulting firms also have intranets where consultants are encouraged to post findings and articles. Why not do so? Partners looking for consultants with specific expertise may staff you on their projects.

Self-training

If you have looked for new projects, done all the available marketing work, and tried to find internal studies to work on, then you still need to keep yourself busy. This is a great time for self-training. Look over your development goals for the year and take steps to pursue them. For example, is your goal to learn Visual Basic? Buy yourself a book and spend six hours a day reading and doing the exercises rigorously. In two weeks or less, you will be reasonably proficient at Visual Basic. (Keep the extra two hours to continue to network for other internal and external opportunities.) Do you want to gain expertise in the energy field? Spend the time reading trade journals, taking notes, and scheduling time with your firm's energy experts to pick their brains.

Visit **Vault Europe's Consulting Career Channel** at www.Vault.com/Europe for insider firm profiles, employee surveys of consultants in Europe, job listings, expert consulting career advice, insider salary information and more.

VAULT CAREER LIBRARY 125

The Consulting Career Path

CHAPTER 9

Training for Consultants

A career in consulting is attractive for many reasons, but few of these are as important to jobseekers as the amount of training they will receive. Unlike industries such as consumer products or pharmaceuticals, where companies funnel investment dollars into product design and research & development, the consulting industry's largest expenditure (apart from staff salaries and overhead) is training. Every year, consulting firms allocate as much as 20 percent of their revenues to internal training programmes, and consultants reap the benefits. It is not uncommon for a consultant to spend four to eight weeks per year attending firm-sponsored classes, taking computer-based training programmes (CBTs), and studying industry-related literature to improve their performance on the job.

The training requirements in consulting are, by any measure, extensive, and employees who hail from top-ranked universities and prestigious firms find the ongoing skill development not only to be personally satisfying, but also valuable. Headhunters and recruiters for FTSE 100 companies realise how much training consultants receive, and they are willing to pay top dollar for people who have spent considerable time developing their skills.

Orientation training

Over the course of their careers, consultants will encounter two general categories of training: orientation and ongoing training. Orientation training begins soon after new recruits walk in the door and greet their assigned human resource representatives. In large firms, most of the orientation training actually occurs in a distant location: after new recruits fill out reams of paperwork at their home office, they board a plane and fly to the firm's massive training campus. Once they check into their assigned rooms, attend a welcome meeting, and spend some time getting to know their "classmates" from around the world, they begin a programme that will last anywhere from one to four weeks, depending on the firm.

Orientation training is notoriously rigorous and exhausting. New recruits spend most of their days working in teams, meeting with firm executives who pose as clients, attending lectures, learning computer code and completing CBTs. Consulting firms spend millions of pounds each year to prepare new recruits for their first few projects and they make sure that, by the end of the training,

Visit **Vault Europe's Consulting Career Channel** at **www.Vault.com/Europe** for insider firm profiles, employee surveys of consultants in Europe, job listings, expert consulting career advice, insider salary information and more.

V/\ULT CAREER LIBRARY 127

employees understand just how strenuous consulting can be. Consulting firms do budget in time for rest and relaxation, but such time pales in comparison to the hard work and countless hours of team-based learning. Regardless, most new consultants, despite feeling worn out at the end of each day, find the experience very gratifying. Orientation training may be a rude awakening, but it offers many perks. Where else can recent university graduates work with people from around the world, build lasting friendships, and be paid large sums of money to attend class?

Ongoing training

Once consultants get acclimated to living in hotels and working with clients, training requirements re-emerge as part of their ongoing development. Every year experienced consultants complete a curriculum of computer training, industry-specific seminars, management workshops and a host of other training programmes designed to complement on-the-job learning.

Aside from making consultants better at what they do, ongoing training also functions as a tool to gauge how ready employees are for promotion. Indeed, many firms will not promote an employee unless he first completes the required curriculum for that particular year. Consultants, therefore, have a two-part incentive for completing their ongoing training requirements. Not only do they hope to become better consultants, but they want very much to rise through the ranks, make more money and have greater responsibility.

Consulting Job Descriptions

Consulting titles vary by firm. Common entry-level titles for recent university grads include associate, consultant and analyst. Typical titles for experienced hires or post-MBAs include associate, senior associate and senior consultant. Distinctions between management titles exist as well — for example: manager, senior manager, director, senior director, managing director, partner, principal, senior partner, managing partner and partner-in-charge.

Analysts and associates

Trying to define and describe the role of a consultant is far from easy. In other professions — lawyer, doctor, accountant — the title says it all. Consultants, however, find themselves explaining their job to people throughout their careers. The individual experience of a consultant varies on firm style, specialisation, geographic differences and the many roles within a project. Initially, the analyst (university graduates) and associate (post-MBA) roles involve different skill sets. However, the differences between a second-year analyst and a new associate are less pronounced.

The analyst role

Analysts are selected for inquiring minds, quantitative aptitude and willingness to learn, rather than any specific industry or functional experience. Most consulting firms offer training programmes, but the main learning occurs on the job. Analysts come to play more important roles within the firm as they gain experience.

Analysts gather and analyse data, draw conclusions from their analyses and pull their results into "stories" the team presents to the client. When client members are involved in the team, an analyst might also manage the client's work on the team to some extent. Take advantage of such circumstances as your opportunity to shine.

The associate role

The associate role evolves rapidly as the consultant gets up to speed and earns the confidence of a more senior consultant. At the beginning, the associate's role might differ from the analyst's if the associate is on an accelerated career track; otherwise, the first year can look identical. A year or so later, however, the associate manages the team's work (client members and analysts) and day-to-day client relationships.

Visit **Vault Europe's Consulting Career Channel** at www.Vault.com/Europe for insider firm profiles, employee surveys of consultants in Europe, job listings, expert consulting career advice, insider salary information and more.

VAULT CAREER LIBRARY   129

She or he generates hypotheses, analyses phases and structures (and occasionally delivers) presentations at client review meetings.

Career Progression in Consulting: Promotion Profile

While job titles at consulting firms differ, the levels and promotion path across firms are remarkably similar: entry-level/undergraduate (analyst), mid-level/MBA (associate), management-level (manager) and the director/partner-level. The primary purpose of each role in your career is to prepare for the next.

Analysts spend their first two or three years learning the consulting ropes. They join projects that span multiple industries, functions and technologies. They start to build reputations for being reliable, spectacular, insightful, or quick. They also start to understand what areas of specialisation they prefer.

Analysts typically spend two to three years at consulting firms before getting an MBA or abandoning the field altogether. Some consulting firms now promote leading analysts directly to the associate level. At some of the top consulting firms (Bain, BCG and McKinsey, for instance) the typical analyst path includes business school before promotion to associate. In rare cases, a sterling analyst is given the option of promotion without business school. In other firms (e.g., Monitor), analysts routinely win promotions to associate after two to three years (or fewer if the candidate has previous work experience). Among the Big Four's IT consulting practices, an MBA is not necessarily a prerequisite for promotion. In fact, the pursuit of an MBA may be encouraged or discouraged, depending on the consultant's area of specialisation.

Associate consultants focus on their desired specialisation almost immediately. During this time, they establish themselves as experts in their chosen areas of focus. They also begin to learn management skills, as they are responsible for managing the team's results and activities hands-on. Networking — both within and outside the firm — becomes increasingly important, because associates will often have to work with other consulting teams (e.g., re-engineering team working with IT team, or working with another consulting firm for the same client).

After one-and-a half to four years as an associate, the next promotion is generally to manager. Consultants at this level manage and develop the day-to-day relationship with key client personnel. They also manage the team's activities in an official capacity. The key differences in this role are the need to step back from the details more often and to manage staff. Unlike the associate who manages the tangibles, managers oversee the team, resolve major issues and make key decisions.

Following manager comes the senior manager position (again, all titles vary by firm), where the consultant begins developing more off-engagement relationships with clients and prospecting for new business. At this stage, the senior manager is also given a broader range of projects to oversee at a higher level. Networking at this level is especially important, since many firms eventually ask their other lines of business to evaluate your partnership worthiness. Also, a large part of partnership status depends on the amount of business you are able to build.

The ultimate aspiration of a career consultant is to achieve the partner (or principal) position. This level requires building and maintaining client relationships and developing the intellectual capital of the firm. Most consultancies operate as partnerships. A promotion to partner normally involves a hefty increase in compensation, as partners contribute directly to the firm's profits. Many firms have upped the ante by lowering their partners' base salaries and tying compensation more directly to how much the partner sells. This creates a strong incentive for the partner to sell new work, though it also creates lots of pressure and sometimes competition among partners.

Some partnerships also have the equivalent of a director position. The director normally declines taking the risks and rewards associated with partnership, but shares the same responsibilities.

Feedback culture

Feedback culture is a major concept among consultancies and will take some getting used to when you start working in one.

The most common approach is a concept known as 360 degree feedback, where you are required to assess everybody within a project, both your superiors and subordinates, on terms like performance, attitude, ability and team spirit. Feedback sessions are carried out after finishing major projects and reviewed and the end of each year of employment. The results of these feedback sessions are the main determinant of your ability to progress within the organisation and what projects you are staffed on. They will also be the key inputs towards the size of your bonus.

Although honesty and openness are highly regarded, the process of feedback can be quite political and gruesome as you will invariably hear good and bad things about yourself from others. However, most consultants appreciate the constructive critique voiced in the feedback reviews as well as the positive effect they have on the quality of the people in consulting. Constant feedback assures that you are only keeping the best of the crop and that deadweight is quickly identified.

In some consultancies (i.e. BCG, Monitor), poor reviews in the feedback sessions result in the person being put on a 'test case' in which the performance of that particular individual will be monitored closely. This offers the underperformer an opportunity to redeem himself by performing according to or above the expectations but can also result in a invitation to leave the company if the required targets are not met.

Internships in Consulting

Many of you are reading this guide as a fresher or second year in university, a recent or first-year MBA, or a graduate student with more than a year left in your degree programme. In these cases, you will be looking for an internship. Simply put, an internship is a temporary position, where consulting firms hire students and other employees for a specified period of time. In addition, because so many of the interns are typically students, and students do not take classes during the summer, most consulting internships occur during the summer months.

For the most part, a consulting internship isn't all that different from the entry-level consulting you would get after you earn your degree. Still, there are a few distinctions worth noting to applicants.

Why internships exist

Most of the large consulting firms have an annual summer internship programme. One reason is that summer internships are a highly effective form of recruiting for everyone involved. A summer internship is a chance for the firm to evaluate you for a couple of months on the job before choosing to extend you a full-time offer. It is also a golden, extended opportunity for the firm to sell you on its interesting projects, work-life balance, and culture. Finally, interns are an incredibly effective form of word-of-mouth advertising. If you have a good experience at the firm, you will no doubt tell all of your classmates about how great the firm is and why they should work there.

In addition, consulting interns are a source of cost-efficient labour for the firm. For instance, interns often are paid less than their full-time equivalents. Even though an undergrad intern might do the work of a first-year analyst for a summer, she or he would probably get paid a little less per month than would the first-year analyst. In addition, hiring a consultant for a summer is cheaper for the firm than bringing on a permanent hire.

That said, the internship is a fantastic opportunity for the employee for a number of reasons. The biggest advantage is that an internship gives the student a great inside track to a full-time offer. In most internship

Visit **Vault Europe's Consulting Career Channel** at **www.Vault.com/Europe** for insider firm profiles, employee surveys of consultants in Europe, job listings, expert consulting career advice, insider salary information and more.

VAULT CAREER LIBRARY **133**

programmes, the highest performing interns are given an offer to join the firm on a full-time basis after graduation.

A typical summer internship

Most consulting summer internships last 8-12 weeks. A number of summer internship programmes start with a week of training to start; typical topics include firm history and values, problem solving, technology training (PowerPoint and Excel for management consultants and systems and programming tools for technology consultants), and presentation skills. If you are interning with a large consulting firm, you will probably have some sort of formalised interactive classroom training along these lines. The smaller firms will often train you on the job instead.

During the first week, an HR professional at the firm will attempt to staff each of the interns, attempting to match the available supply of projects with the interns' interests. Not all interns are staffed immediately, but because they are a priority in the staffing queue, most are staffed within the first two weeks.

The projects are, for the most part, real engagements. As the intern, chances are good that your start date won't coincide with the project kick-off, so you really could join the project at any time.

Typical tasks for the undergraduate intern are not that different from those of the first-year analyst, and the job of the MBA summer intern is similar to that of the first-year associate. The main difference is that because the intern is a temporary hire, his or her work needs to be completed within a defined period of time that may not coincide with the actual project completion. So, by and large, interns will be assigned clearly segmentable project work, like the secondary research of 15 competitors, a small market sizing spreadsheet model, or a specific set of PowerPoint slides. MBA interns might take on additional responsibility, such as more extensive financial modelling. (Please refer to the "On the Job" section of this guide for a description of typical tasks.)

Many internship programmes involve at least one performance review, at the end of the summer. Some programmes have a mid-summer review as well. This can be helpful because it gives the intern a chance to improve his or her work before offers are made. If you don't have a formal review planned as part of your internship, be proactive in asking for one.

Finally, since as an intern you are still technically a recruit, you will likely be wined and dined. Perks include free fine dining, events and concerts. In recent years, firms have scaled back these perks considerably for cost reasons, but interns will probably get a nice meal or two during the summer regardless.

Landing a summer internship in consulting

The recruiting process for summer internships is identical to that for full-time offers. The only difference is timing. The summer internship recruiting cycle typically starts in January, whereas often consulting firms hire for full-time in the autumn. Be sure to check with your university's career office for timing and procedures.

Be warned that in an economic slowdown, there are fewer available internships for undergraduates and MBAs. A compounding effect is the seasonality of the consulting industry. The summer months typically result in the lowest spending on consultants of any part of the year. Keep in mind that internships are more competitive than permanent jobs. Some firms are recruiting the vast majority of full-time hires from their internship classes.

Treat the consulting internship job search like an off-campus job search. Do the research on firms and contact your targets to see if they are recruiting interns. Also, if you have flexibility in your campus schedule, see if you can work during the spring or autumn instead, when there will be fewer students competing for scarce internship spots. If the firm is local, see if you can work part-time.

Tips on being an effective summer intern

Not all internships result in offers so we recommend you focus on making the most out of your summer internship in all other ways.

- Ask to be put on an engagement with travel. You really want to make sure you will like consulting, so push yourself. If you try to get on a project with no travel, you will not have a realistic picture of consulting (since that would be the exception, not the norm).

- Collect business cards. You will be meeting lots of consultants, and it will difficult to remember them all. Try to grab their business card at some point and make a few notes on the back. In the future, you can touch base with them and have a few titbits to remind them who you are.

- Attend as many social events as possible. Treat the summer as one long networking event. You want to meet as many consultants of all levels at firm, and you will want to stay in touch with the other interns you meet.

- Set up Friday one-on-one meetings. Again, you are building your network. Try to meet up with a wide range of consultants, including partners. Friday is a great day for this, because consultants tend to be in their home office on Fridays. Grab coffee with some of the newer consultants to get the inside scoop on the firm.

Visit **Vault Europe's Consulting Career Channel** at **www.Vault.com/Europe** for insider firm profiles, employee surveys of consultants in Europe, job listings, expert consulting career advice, insider salary information and more.

VAULT CAREER LIBRARY 135

Performance assessment

Performance assessment is a critical tool for your career development and the firm's success. Usually, someone one level above you on "larger" projects reviews your performance at the end of the project or phase. (By most definitions, a "larger" project involves a minimum of 80 hours, though the exact figure differs by firm.) Some firms require self-assessments as well, and some will have the so-called 360 degree review in which you will be asked to review your subordinates and your managers. The reviews are designed to evaluate your progress and any development needs you might have.

Most firms conduct official reviews of all consultants on an annual or semi-annual basis. Management goes off-site and/or holds meetings that can last several days. While each firm's practices vary, most generally use this time to measure your performance against your peers. Based on where you fall in the lineup, management determines your salary increase and evaluates your readiness for promotion.

To ensure you fall near the top of the list, document and self-promote every success or instance in which you excelled beyond expectations. Solicit your clients for letters of gratitude or recommendation for your personnel file. Train yourself in areas of interest to you and let it be known that you are an "expert." Conduct research and analysis studies on little-known fields within your industry or service line, and (just out of the goodness of your heart) share the information with your colleagues. Just as you did extra credit work in university, make public the initiatives you introduced to differentiate yourself from your peers. In short, going the extra mile in all aspects of your career gets you noticed.

Your image can help or hurt you. The most competent consultant can be overlooked if his or her peers are not as shy about showcasing their best work. An enthusiastic attitude can only work for you, yet you might feel uncomfortable about boasting, or feel adamantly that your work should speak for itself. If so, find some other way to let your competence and high standards of excellence be known to your superiors.

Your performance is measured by criteria similar to those first used to hire you — analytical and quantitative skills, teamwork and leadership. As you progress, the evaluation emphasis shifts toward your people management skills and client relationship capabilities, including your ability to sell. While matching your perceptions of your performance with your managers, address your development needs, organise your training and set your goals.

Office politics

Office politics is a fact of life in any corporate environment, though the consulting industry is no worse, and in many ways better, than other industries in this regard. Frequent reviews and performance assessments, a reliance on teamwork and the relative lack of hierarchical frills all help downplay office politics in the consulting environment. Perhaps the most politically charged aspect of the consulting life is the competition to be staffed on engagements.

Consulting firms all have an official process by which consultants are staffed on projects. This may be done through a central staffing office or by a senior consultant at the firm. However, all consulting firms have a parallel black market, an unofficial system where consultants are either chosen directly for projects by their directors, or where consultants network and approach the leaders of their desired engagements directly.

Understand the unofficial process from the start and play the game with the best of them — after all, your projects and the directors for whom you work can make or break your consulting experience. Getting on choice assignments means less probability of being pigeonholed unwillingly and a greater probability of visibility.

Project staffing addresses conflicting needs from various constituencies. On the one hand, the firm wants associates and analysts to gain broad exposure to different industries and project types. On the other hand, both clients and partners prefer to staff projects with consultants who have some experience in the area, and directors often request specific consultants whom they have found reliable on prior engagements. Moreover, clients' needs sometimes take precedence, depending on market demands. This complicated situation results in elaborate compromises between your firm's management and the client, which means that your personal needs are sometimes overlooked.

To stack the assignment cards in your favour, tap unofficial sources of information about upcoming projects. The best source of information is management (from either your current or previous studies) or your mentor. Learn about projects that you would potentially want to work on, and express an interest up front to these senior people. Tell as many people as you can about your areas of interest. When a relevant study comes up, ask them to remember you as an enthusiastic team member. While remembering you does not guarantee you a position, it certainly helps.

You can also volunteer to help with knowledge development or intellectual capital work being done within your firm. Practice development leaders constantly search for additional help and jump at the chance to get willing consultants involved. In addition to developing your understanding of the industry, volunteering exposes you to senior consultants.

Visit **Vault Europe's Consulting Career Channel** at **www.Vault.com/Europe** for insider firm profiles, employee surveys of consultants in Europe, job listings, expert consulting career advice, insider salary information and more.

VAULT CAREER LIBRARY **137**

Additionally, you gain valuable skills and knowledge. As your value to the firm increases, your value to clients also increases, which means your negotiating power increases proportionally.

Mentors: Top-level Backing

Soon after orientation at your firm, expect to be assigned to a formal mentor. Your mentor is responsible for your success within the firm. Recognize the usefulness of this relationship from the start. Your mentor is responsible for your development, so speak candidly with him or her about your career aspirations, assignment preferences and development needs. Your mentor also acts as an informal communication channel with you and other management. He or she relays impressions of your performance and how others in the firm perceive you. Think of your mentor alternately as your champion, spy, ally and bouncer within your firm.

In addition to mentors, many firms offer "buddies" – professionals who are slightly more experienced than you (often a year or so more advanced) and available to assist with day-to-day details, like how to fill out an expense sheet. Often, these buddies are good first-line mentors. While they might offer less insight because of their limited work experience, they make excellent sounding boards, generally have more time than managers and usually want to help you.

If both your assigned mentor and buddy lack time, information or attention for you, consider seeking other mentors. Still, maintain an "official" assigned mentor/buddy relationship, unless your chemistry leads to unbearable resentment or negativity. (It only helps you to have more people in your corner.) Develop an informal mentor network with those who specialize in an area of interest to you or share some other commonality. Seek out those with whom you find communication, rapport, and understanding to be natural.

Just remember that your mentor/buddy is not necessarily your friend. Indeed, some prefer to keep mentoring relationships separate from personal and/or professional friendships, and you might feel it is better to keep the relationship's capacity strictly official.

Exit Strategies

Bain often calls its consulting positions a "springboard" to an exciting career. Indeed, if you are not excited about the idea of selling work 100 percent of the time as a consulting partner, you will eventually be leaving consulting.

What you might do later

As we mentioned before, many analysts in consulting move on to business school or abandon the field altogether. Some of them return to their employer (the lucky ones get tuition paid for), while others move to other consulting firms or even change careers. If you're an analyst interested in graduate study, take the time to consider the possibility of a different graduate programme. It is easy to get caught up in thinking that business school is the next obvious thing, because it most definitely is. Simply make sure that you wouldn't be more interested in law school, a teaching qualification, or a PhD in your favourite university subject.

A lot of associates who leave their firms take positions in corporate strategy, marketing or business development. Some find employment with former clients. Not all associates who leave their firms abandon consulting, however; many of them move to other consulting firms in an attempt to "trade up," in the form of a different brand name or a faster promotion to a better title.

Leaving gracefully

Whatever you choose to do to follow your days at your current consulting firm, be it another consulting firm or graduate study, you never, ever want to burn your bridges, no matter how bitter you may be or how anxious you are to leave. What if your new job turns out to be a disaster and you want to return to your old firm? What if the market for new PhDs in English fizzles when you graduate? Suppose you graduate from the MBA programme in a recession?

What if you need a reference — or even a job — from your old employer?

When you have secured your new position or admission to university, speak individually to your official and unofficial mentors in the firm-all of them that mean something to you. If they don't know already, tell them about your new opportunity and why you have chosen it. Then, explain how grateful you are for the opportunities you have had at your current firm, and especially for that person's generosity and guidance. The week you leave, try to schedule a couple of key one-on-one lunches. Even if you are excited to leave the firm, you want to make sure people remember you. When you get to your new destination, send your updated contact information to your key sponsors at your old firm. Try to keep in touch by phone or e-mail once every six months or so to start.

Visit **Vault Europe's Consulting Career Channel** at **www.Vault.com/Europe** for insider firm profiles, employee surveys of consultants in Europe, job listings, expert consulting career advice, insider salary information and more.

VAULT CAREER LIBRARY **139**

You may never go back to your former employer again, and that's fine. But having taken the small steps to exit with grace, you will always be able to call on your former employer as a reference.

Get the inside edge for your consulting career.

Vault Consulting Employee Surveys – Find out what life is like on the job at top consulting firms with Vault's exclusive consultant surveys.

Vault Consulting Career Ghannel – See job listings at top consulting firms, read insider advice on consulting careers, research top firms and more.

Go to the Vault Europe Consulting Career Channel at www.Vault.com/Europe

Our Survey Says: The Consulting Lifestyle

CHAPTER 10

For people considering a career in consulting, few factors matter as much as the lifestyle. The demands of heavy travel, long workdays and months of living out of suitcases are enough to drive many jobseekers away. For others, however, the thrill of the constantly changing business environments, the frequent flyer miles and the chance to work with new project teams are too much to pass up. Consulting may be a grind, but it remains a prestigious way to make a living, a great training ground for senior management positions in FTSE 250 companies and a ticket to see the world.

Salary and benefits

Relative to other career paths, consulting salaries for undergraduates are very attractive. You might earn anywhere from £25,000 to £40,000 in the first year, plus any sign-on bonuses, which can range from £2,000 to £15,000.

Salaries for MBA hires are in flux. Until the downturn in the economy, prestigious firms like McKinsey, BCG, and Accenture had been pushing offers to newly minted MBAs into the £90,000 range, with sign-on bonuses as high as £40,000. In some cases, MBA candidates were getting their entire business school tuition paid for — on top of all the money thrown at them on Day One. (In 2002, the downturn in the economy had depressed market base salaries closer to £60,000 and bonuses to around £5,000. Since then, they have improved but there are significant differences between firms — and you should consider the likely future income as well as the starting offer — partners' drawing in Deloitte averaged £615,000 in 2004/5.)

The focus for new recruits quickly shifts to other monetary factors, such as raises. Here again, a career in consulting outpaces nearly every other option. At top consulting firms, standard raises often start in the 10 percent range and escalate into the 20 to 25 percent range for high performers. Consultants also stand to benefit from profit-sharing programmes, year-end bonuses or overtime pay, depending on the firm.

The benefit packages are icing on the cake, and new recruits rarely complain. It is completely reasonable to expect full coverage in areas such as medical/dental, life and disability, adoption and elder care assistance and pension schemes. Add in substantial holiday time, gym discounts, and discounts at local shops, and the temptation to take a consulting job is all the more difficult to resist.

Visit **Vault Europe's Consulting Career Channel** at www.Vault.com/Europe for insider firm profiles, employee surveys of consultants in Europe, job listings, expert consulting career advice, insider salary information and more.

V/\ULT CAREER LIBRARY 141

Per diems make a difference

One commonly overlooked facet of consulting is per diems, which represent the extra pay that a consultant receives while staffed on an out-of-town assignment. Consulting firms realise that when a consultant is away on assignment, cost of living factors are higher than would be normal. Out-of-town projects require that you stay in hotels or leased apartments and spend long hours at the client site, making it hard to perform simple tasks like shopping for food or doing your laundry. Consulting firms pick up the slack for you. They may pay you a daily amount that takes into consideration where you've been assigned and the added daily costs associated with being away from home.

Per diems are given to you as part of your expenses, and they can range from £20 to £40 per day, depending on the firm and your project's location. Over the course of a two-week period, an allotment of per diems can add a few hundred pounds to your bottom line. Over the course of a year, your salary can grow by more than £6,000 — a nice way for firms to even the playing field for consultants who are working far from home.

Not all firms use the per diem option, and some firms have different policies, so be sure to check with your firm's HR accountants to understand not only what the policies are but also how you can benefit the most.

Hilton, sweet home

Although some consultants are lucky enough to stay in leased flats while on assignment, most end up in hotel rooms where the quality of life can grow stale very quickly. Project managers usually decide where the team will stay. If you have to stay in hotels, the brand or chain will be less important than the proximity to the client site. The closer the hotel is to the client site, the better.

New members of a project team check into their hotel rooms after landing at the airport. Once bags are unloaded, the trek to the client site begins. Work starts immediately, and your hotel room quickly becomes a place where you spend very little time. Nonetheless, everything in the hotel, every detail, begins to take on a much greater importance than you ever expected. Size of the room. Sitting area. TV stations. Fax capabilities and location of electrical outlets (for your laptop). In-house restaurants. Workout facilities. Food quality.

Experienced consultants are experts at hotel living, and when they have time at night, they are very picky about what they eat. One of the options they try to avoid, whenever possible, is room service. Getting out of the hotel, venturing to new restaurants and trying new things at night are great ways to enhance the life of a consulting engagement. If you only see the client site and the inside of your hotel room, it will wear on you. Get outside, take a drive, see the locale in which you are living. Change of scenery makes a big difference.

One fringe benefit of hotel living, for those who stay in hotels often, is the loyalty scheme. Under this system, you earn points for every pound spent, and after accumulating enough points you can "pay for" free nights. Many hotel chains offer this benefit, and its popularity among consultants is growing. In fact, many consultants obsess over how many points they've accumulated, keeping close count of just how many holidays they will take without ever having to pay for hotel rooms. Points can add up, so pay attention to them. They can make an out-of-town assignment much easier to handle.

Planes, trains, and automobiles

Most consulting firms have scaled back the time their employees spend away from the home office. The competition to offer new recruits an attractive work/life balance is much fiercer than it was 10 years ago; some firms now practically guarantee that consultants will spend Friday at the home office. Even so, consulting is still about travel, whether to a client site, home again after a long week in a distant city, or to training facilities around the world.

Frequent flyer points ease the burden. Spend a few years in consulting, and the miles you earn will cover nearly every personal trip that you take during your employment as a consultant.

Another concern is how you will commute to the client site once you arrive. Will you have a hire car? Will you travel to the site by train? Do you have to share a car with other project team members? These issues impact your quality of life once you reach the client site. You may have to share a hire car in your first few years on the job. Ask.

Take a long holiday

One major perk of consulting is extensive holiday time. Most firms understand how demanding the job can be, and they know that you will need plenty of time each year to decompress.

Actually scheduling a holiday is another story. Consulting projects can have a life of their own, and project managers need key resources when you least expect it. Planning a holiday on short notice usually won't work, because your project manager needs time to

Visit **Vault Europe's Consulting Career Channel** at www.Vault.com/Europe for insider firm profiles, employee surveys of consultants in Europe, job listings, expert consulting career advice, insider salary information and more.

VAULT CAREER LIBRARY 143

fill your spot while you are gone. If you want to take a holiday in the consulting industry, you need to plan it far ahead and remind people of your approaching holiday to avoid any confusion.

Don't Burn Out

By Hannah Im

The daily life of a consultant is both exciting and dynamic. Still, consulting is a fairly high stress job: the travelling, the long hours, elongated separation from loved ones, cramped spaces, reams of paper, the ever-present computer screen, and sleeplessness. Here, Hannah Im, a former consultant, shares her experiences with the consulting workload.

I remember when I got my first job out of university — consulting with a big firm. My peers were jealous. Consulting sounded so glamorous to them. At the time, I was a liberal arts double major. I knew nothing about business and even less about consulting. I only knew, based on the education I got from my peers, that I was embarking on an exciting, dynamic career path.

For the first few years, I learned so much. My "exciting and dynamic" expectations were fuelled each day with new challenges, new acquaintances, stimulating discussions, etc. Consulting gave me an intellectual titillation my English and Asian studies never offered. My analysis up to that point had been strictly academic. I blossomed. I networked my way around the firm and found great mentors, team-mates, and role models. My motivation came from many forces and factors. Every day I awoke, I commuted or flew with the excitement of a child anticipating Christmas.

At the same time, I struggled a great deal. Most of my colleagues had studied pertinent majors, or boasted impressive internships, or hung MBA degrees on their cubicle walls. On the contrary, I was just stepping into the corporate world. When I decided to look for a job in the last months of senior year, I only knew I wanted to work. So I networked for jobs where I had contacts, not where I thought I would succeed as a consultant.

Since the partners hired me on the spot, I naively believed my qualifications were adequate. But on my first day of work, I knew I stood at a disadvantage. I needed to learn not just about consulting, but also about every industry our clients represented. I also had to learn basic business and technology concepts. "Operating system" and "DOS" were foreign words to me, as were "stockholder," "cost benefit analysis," and "business process reengineering." It was obvious to me the partners made a mistake in recruiting me. I clearly did not belong here.

Additionally, I graduated from a women's university and, for the first time in four years, I had to interact with male peers again. It took me some time to figure out how most of them had matured since high school. It also took me some time to understand the politics between men and women, the different positions, the different lines of business, and client-consultant relationships. I hardly slept because I was so busy trying to learn, keep up and prove I was just as good.

On top of that, my enthusiasm and apparent inability to decline requests kept my in-box mountainous. Of course, I did not mind taking on more projects than any other first-year consultant. Each project represented another opportunity to learn, to demonstrate my competence and to meet more people. As a result, I worked harder than everyone else — not just in volume, but also in an effort to learn fast enough and to do a good job. It was easy enough to maintain for a while; after all, I was young and bright. I was earning high praise and assigned to the firm's biggest clients and most stimulating projects. Yet, I was constantly nervous that the mistake of my hiring would become evident.

I was caught up in a cycle I didn't know how to break. I spent two to four days a week at the office until sunrise, only to go home for a quick shower before my next meeting. Eventually, my adrenaline dried up and dread overtook me. I stopped walking into my office with a smile. I was burned out.

In order to recover, I took six months off from consulting and went into banking. In banking, I found routine. I found safety. I found sanity. But during that time, I also found dryness, micro-management and resulting frustration. I needed the diversity and stimulation of consulting again. I wrestled with my conscience. Leaving a company after less than a year seemed somehow wrong to me. Yet, I felt strongly that six months was all I needed to restore myself. So I took charge of my career again and networked my way back into consulting. Within a week of my deciding to transition back, I found a position. I felt like I was breathing fresh air again.

Throughout my consulting career, my most valuable lesson came from burn out. I never want to go through it again. It was the darkest period of my life. From that point forward, I learned how to monitor myself and my environment — the stress, the travel, the assignments, the politics, etc. This time, rather than blossoming, I matured and found confidence in my work. I forced myself to feel

Visit **Vault Europe's Consulting Career Channel** at www.Vault.com/Europe for insider firm profiles, employee surveys of consultants in Europe, job listings, expert consulting career advice, insider salary information and more.

VAULT CAREER LIBRARY **145**

comfortable being firm with my time constraints and managed my time and my relationships better. I managed my projects better too.

Burning out can be detrimental to your career. You forget what your priorities mean to you, because work becomes your ultimate priority. You forget how important it is to care for yourself, because work becomes you. You lose yourself, the quality of your work declines and your reputation for quality evaporates as well. My personal consulting motto is, "the only promotion in consulting is self-promotion." Your image and reputation are pivotal in our profession. They are also very delicate and often difficult to repair, once diminished.

I hope none of you ever go through a burn out experience. If you do, I hope you come out stronger for it and find yourself a better person for it. In the meantime, I recommend taking classes in time management, project management, stress management and negotiation. If you are uncomfortable taking classes, devise a system that works for you.

I also recommend you find ways to moderate your stress and intolerance for the little peccadilloes that are sure to vex you. For some of you, that means exercise or creative releases. For others, it means finding expressions of your spirituality or spending time with those you love most. However you choose to temper your work with your personal needs is up to you, obviously. Just be sure to be healthy and take care of yourself.

annah Im specialises in business operations, specifically process improvement/ reengineering and risk management.

Hannah Im has been a consultant throughout her career. She specialises in business operations, specifically process improvement/reengineering and risk management.

Work hard, play hard

Reputable firms spare no expense for the hard working employees who drive their revenue growth. Consulting is all about working hard and playing hard, and consultants play very hard.

That said, your project's entertainment budget will depend on how much work your partners sell, the price of the work and the negotiating skills of your partners. Generally, you can tell how big the fun budget will be by the type of client. Government clients aren't big spenders. Expect the project dinners to be middle-of-the-road, infrequent and no fun. Work in financial services or pharmaceuticals, however, and the budgets are much better, sometimes lavish. But don't worry too much about the project budgets. If your project doesn't have a lot of fun money, your firm often chips in for your enjoyment.

Consulting firms are, by and large, very friendly places where people form long-lasting relationships. Partying with your peers and colleagues is all part of the experience, and consultants (partners included) party a lot. Join a consulting firm and you will reap the social perks. Just remember to take a breather from time to time, because too many nights with just four hours of sleep will take their toll.

Maintaining a personal life from afar

Many new consultants are not prepared for the difficulty of maintaining friendships and personal relationships from the road. You vow to stay in touch with your friends, but then you find yourself exhausted on the weekends and unable to schedule time for a personal call to a friend during the week. As a result, you can lose touch with your friends. Moreover, it can be very hard to maintain a relationship with a significant other, let alone a family, when you are away from home three nights a week.

That said, if you are going to make this career work for you, you will need to take responsibility for keeping close to loved ones. While consulting has its unexpected crises, the schedule can be predictable. So plan ahead!

• Every Monday, for example, schedule what fun or intimate event you are going to have with your spouse, significant other or family. Also on Monday, pick one or two friends and call them that evening to make plans for Thursday, Friday, or Saturday, whatever you have available.

• You might want to consider setting up a standing appointment with a set of friends, to make sure you keep in touch. How about meeting with your closest friends every third Sunday of the month for brunch?

• Also, if you haven't already, get used to relying on your mobile phone as your true source of connection with others. Perhaps you have lots of friends that you want to stay in touch with, or you prioritise speaking with your family every day. Carve out bits of time here and there to call them using your cell phone. Good times include: in the car driving to and from the client, during lunch, or right after dinner. Remember that you only need ten minutes to speak with people. During the next flight delay you have, make your calls.

Visit **Vault Europe's Consulting Career Channel** at **www.Vault.com/Europe** for insider firm profiles, employee surveys of consultants in Europe, job listings, expert consulting career advice, insider salary information and more.

VAULT CAREER LIBRARY 147

- Another lifesaver is online bill payment services. Check with your bank to see if you can automate as many monthly bills as possible. This will allow you to spend less time on the weekends doing paperwork and more time with the people in your life.

- Need balance? Why not sign up for a weekend art or music programme? Maybe you can attend a weekend class at a local institution.

Sounds too regimented? Take it from a few current and former consultants — it is all too easy to let life slip away. A happy, fulfilling personal life makes a happy consultant.

Days in the Life

CHAPTER 11

It's tough to visualise yourself as a consultant if you haven't been there and done that. Here, we bring you real days in the life of consultants at different levels and at different types of consulting firms. Is this lifestyle for you?

Associate

Greg Schneider is an associate at the London office of a top strategy consulting firm office. He kindly agreed to share a "typical" workday with Vault, noting that no day at any consulting firm can be called typical.

6:15 a.m.: Alarm goes off. I wake up, asking myself why I put "run three times per week" into the team charter. I meet another member of the team, and we hobble out for a jog. At least it's warm out — another advantage of having a project in Barcelona.

7:15 a.m.: Check voice mail. Someone wants a copy of my knowledge building document on managing hyper growth. A co-worker is looking for information about what the partner from my last team is like to work with.

7:30 a.m.: Breakfast with the team. We discuss sport, and a morning meeting we have with the client team (not necessarily in that order). We then head out to the client.

9:00 a.m.: Meet with the client team. We've got an important progress review with the CEO next week, so there's a lot going on. We're helping the client to assess the market potential of an emerging technology. Today's meeting concerns what kind of presentation would be most effective, although we have trouble staying off tangents about the various analyses that we've all been working on. The discussion is complicated by the fact that some key data is not yet available. We elect to go with a computer-based slide show and begin the debate on the content.

10:53 a.m.: Check voice mail. The office is looking for an interviewer for the Insead hell weekend. The partner will be arriving in time for dinner and wants to meet to discuss the progress review. A head-hunter looking for a divisional VP. My wife reminding me to mail off the insurance forms.

11:00 a.m.: I depart with my team-mate for an interview. We meet with an industry expert (a professor from a local university) to discuss industry trends and in particular what the

Visit **Vault Europe's Consulting Career Channel** at **www.Vault.com/Europe** for insider firm profiles, employee surveys of consultants in Europe, job listings, expert consulting career advice, insider salary information and more.

V∧ULT CAREER LIBRARY **149**

prospects are for the type of technology we're looking at. As this is the last interview we plan to do, we are able to check many of our hypotheses. The woman is amazing — we luck out and get some data we need. The bad news is, now we have to figure out what it means.

12:28 p.m.: As I walk back in to the client, a division head I've been working with grabs me and we head to lunch. He wanted to discuss an analysis he'd given me some information for, and in the process I get some interesting perspectives about the difficulties in moving the technology into full production and how much it could cost.

1:30 p.m.: I jump on a quick conference call about an internal knowledge building project I'm working on for the marketing practice. I successfully avoid taking on any additional responsibility.

2:04 p.m.: Begin to work through new data. After discussing the plan of attack with the engagement manager, I dive in. It's a very busy afternoon, but the data is great. I get a couple "a-ha"s — always a good feeling.

3:00 p.m.: Short call with someone from Legal to get an update on the patent search.

6:00 p.m.: Team meeting. The engagement manager pulls the team together to check progress on various fronts and debate some issues prior to heading to dinner with the partner. A quick poll determines that Italian food wins — we leave a voice mail with the details.

6:35 p.m.: Call home and check in with the family. Confirm plans for weekend trip to Dorset. Apologise for forgetting to mail the insurance forms.

7:15 p.m.: The team packs up and heads out to dinner. We meet the partner at the restaurant and have a productive (and calorific) meal working through our plans for the progress review, the new data, what's going on with the client team, and other areas of interest. She suggests some additional uses for the new data, adds her take on our debates, and agrees to raise a couple issues with the CFO, whom she's known for years. She takes a copy of our draft presentation to read after dinner.

9:15 p.m.: Return to hotel. Plug in computer and check e-mail, since I hadn't had a chance all day. While I'm logged in, I download two documents I need from the company database, check the Arsenal score, and see how the client's stock did.

10:10 p.m.: Pre-sleep voice mail check. A client from a previous study is looking for one of the appendices, since he lost his copy. The server will be down for an hour tomorrow night.

10:30 p.m.: Watch Sky instead of going right to sleep, as I know I probably should.

Note: Had this been an in-town study, the following things would have been different: I wouldn't have run with another member of my team, and we'd have substituted a conference call for the dinner meeting, so we could go home instead. Also, I probably wouldn't have watched Sky.

Visit **Vault Europe's Consulting Career Channel** at **www.Vault.com/Europe** for insider firm profiles, employee surveys of consultants in Europe, job listings, expert consulting career advice, insider salary information and more.

VAULT CAREER LIBRARY **151**

Consultant Project Manager

Hans Helbekkmo is a project manager. He kindly agreed to share a "typical" workday with Vault.

6:00 a.m.: Alarm goes off, Monday morning. I take a few seconds to remember that I'm in Lyon, where I've just spent a terrific weekend with my girlfriend. I have to catch an 8:30 flight to Düsseldorf, where I've been working on a project for the past 5 months.

8:15 a.m.: After checking in, I phone up my team and tell them I'll be in around 10. Richard, a first-year consultant, tells me that Jason, the director primarily responsible for the project, left a message that he wanted to see the presentation document for our afternoon meeting with the client board member in charge of our workstream [in planning our schedule]. Otherwise no important messages. I check my voicemail messages and learn that Jason, just returned from holiday, was unaware of our meeting, but he can make it.

9:30 a.m.: Land in Düsseldorf and jump in a cab. While our project requires that we spend at least Monday through Thursday on the client site, I pretty much spend every weekend out of town, either at home in London, travelling to visit friends or family, or simply finding a spot on the map with better weather than the Ruhrgebiet [the Ruhr Valley]. My company covers reasonable travel expenses, which makes life more enjoyable. And I'm now an expert on finding the fastest route through customs/ immigration and getting to the front of the taxi queue in zero time.

10:00 a.m.: Arrive at work. Jason's already in and is discussing the presentation document with Daniel, the other consultant on my team. Jason tells me that Gerhard, the director responsible for the overall client relationship, cannot make the afternoon meeting. Not a disaster — it is very hard to schedule meetings with a board-level client, and I'm perfectly happy bringing just one director along.

10:15 a.m.: I change into a suit and catch up on the conversation. Jason is happy with what we've put together, but he has some detailed questions on a couple of our charts. Daniel shows us an alternative analysis that makes the same points more convincingly. We decide to go with the new slides, and cut down the document a bit to keep it "short and sweet."

10:30 a.m.: Finally time to check my e mail. I have about 20 new messages, mostly personal or process related. A colleague wants to pick my brains on asset/liability management and liquidity management. Gerhard says he wants to discuss Daniel's mid-year review, so I put this into my "to-do" list. Richard already had his review on Friday, so I make a note of talking to him about it later.

11:00 a.m.: While Daniel is working on the document changes, I go through an outline for our final presentation with Jason. We have less than one month left, and I want to get Jason's input. We are working towards a quite comprehensive strategic review. It is very clear what the right solution for the bank is, but we need to put together a detailed explanation of the implications and likely outcomes, so our client can convince the full board to approve our proposed initiatives. Jason agrees with the main contents and level of detail, and he does not have any further suggestions.

Directors typically give the project team full responsibility for developing recommendations and executing the project on a day-to-day basis, which makes my job both challenging and rewarding. We will have a more detailed review once all the interviews and analysis are done and the final document is drafted. For now I just want to make sure we're all on the same track.

12:00 p.m.: Time for lunch — Jason and Daniel decide to grab a sandwich, so I take Richard to the Italian cafe across the street. I ask how his mid-year review went, and he say he's happy with it-no surprises, nothing new was mentioned that I hadn't already discussed with him. He was told to focus on improving his communication and process skills. Richard has a PhD in finance and has just started working for us. I tell him it is typical for someone who's worked in academia for a while to need some time to adjust to the particular demands of our job in terms of client communication. It is sometimes difficult to adapt to the comprehension level of our clients, especially since we tend to have a very strong analytical and theoretical knowledge base, while our clients have a much more practical background. In any case, I'm happy that Richard agrees with our assessment of his performance.

1:00 p.m.: I sit down with Richard to get an update on the database work he's been doing over the past couple of days. We're broadly on track, though we need to get a couple of extra data fields to produce the reports we want to deliver. I ask him to discuss this with the client's systems people and try to find a solution that doesn't produce undue additional workload. We only have a couple of weeks to get the reporting up and running, so I'm a bit worried about our progress. The systems people have been predictably slow in providing us with data, so the result is likely to be some late hours next week. That's the nature of this job — when things go as planned we rarely do more than 50-55 hours a week, but the occasional crunch or hiccup from the client can easily result in 18-hour days. Our company is strongly committed to avoiding long hours, and it is largely my responsibility

Visit **Vault Europe's Consulting Career Channel** at www.Vault.com/Europe for insider firm profiles, employee surveys of consultants in Europe, job listings, expert consulting career advice, insider salary information and more.

VAULT CAREER LIBRARY 153

to make sure this is complied with. This requires careful planning and occasionally standing my ground with clients and project directors, making sure not to commit to unreasonable deliverables.

2:00 p.m.: Jean-Pierre, our main day-to-day client contact, phones me to make sure we're on track for the meeting. I confirm that everything's fine and that we should meet outside the client's office at 5:30. I mail him the latest version of the document.

2:30 p.m.: Daniel has finished the edits. We go through the document one last time. It's a convincing "story" and has the right level of detail.

3:00 p.m.: Jason and I sit down to plan the meeting. The board-level client is likely to have about 45 minutes, and he probably won't have many questions. We decide not to draw too many conclusions when discussing the slides, but rather try to invite discussion and get a sense of where he wants to go with this. The topics we're dealing with have strong political implications, and we need to trust his judgement on how aggressively we should formulate our recommendations. After all, it is our main job to provide content and insight, while the client really remains the expert on internal politics.

3:45 p.m.: I phone up my travel agent to confirm my trip to London next weekend.

5:15 p.m.: Jason and I discuss whether we should bring Richard and Daniel to the meeting. We usually involve junior staff in as many discussions as possible and give them an opportunity to present their own results. However, the meeting is likely to be conducted in German, which would leave Daniel stranded, so we decide not to bring them along.

5:30 p.m.: Jason and I meet up with Jean-Pierre, and the meeting starts on time. I quickly talk the board-level client through the document — in English after all. He agrees with the main messages and says we should state our findings and recommendations very clearly, although this may upset some of the other board members. He says he will try to get a decision on our strategy within two months.

6:15 p.m.: Quick debrief with Jean-Pierre and Jason.

6:30 p.m.: I summarise the meeting for Daniel and Richard and give them due credit for their good work.

7:00 p.m.: Jason jumps on a train back to Frankfurt, and I take my team out for dinner. Düsseldorf has a large selection of terrific Japanese restaurants, and we pick our favourite to celebrate a successful day. The conversation meanders through the Mexican election, U.S. drug policy, quantum computers, and the latest Nick Hornby novel. Shop talk is strictly off-limits during evenings, a policy I've adapted from my previous job managers.

10:00 p.m.: We move on to the Altstadt for a few drinks

11:00 p.m.: I go home to my flat, watch the last half-hour of *Poltergeist* in German, read another chapter of *The Name of The Rose*, where Adso spends five pages musing on the religious justification for his sinful desires — which finally puts me to sleep.

Visit **Vault Europe's Consulting Career Channel** at **www.Vault.com/Europe** for insider firm profiles, employee surveys of consultants in Europe, job listings, expert consulting career advice, insider salary information and more.

VAULT CAREER LIBRARY **155**

MBA-Level Strategy Consultant

Dan is a twenty-eight-year-old recent graduate of a top business school. Dan lives in London and works for a firm generally regarded as one of the top strategic consultancies worldwide. Before business school, Dan worked in operations management for a large healthcare provider. Presently, Dan works in the pharmaceutical industry group at the firm.

5:45 a.m.: The alarm clock rings — it's Monday morning, and I instantly calculate the amount of time I have to get to the airport. I have a very important client meeting at 1 p.m. near Brussels, and a 7:30 a.m. departure. Airport security delays [post 9/11] have been terrible, so I have to allow more time.

6:10 a.m.: Checking email from my laptop while shaving, I look through an email from Rolph, my engagement manager at ABC Pharmaceuticals in Belgium. The request is for clarification on a section of the financial model I created over the weekend. While packing my suitcase, I dash off a few sentences to explain key assumptions in the statement of cash flows. The e-mail only takes a few minutes, but I'm worried it could make me miss my flight.

6:28 a.m.: I get on the Tube [London's subway system] for what's normally a 35-minute ride to Heathrow airport from my Hammersmith apartment. Normally, a taxi ride would be better since I could open up my laptop and do some work, but I have learned from hard experience that the potential variance on traffic jams is just too risky. The Tube is a little slower, but a lot more predictable. I get a cup of coffee from an underground vendor just as the trolley car pulls in to the station.

6:57 a.m.: The Tube pulls up to Terminal 4. I'm really cutting it close. Above ground again off the tube, I check my voice mail — seven messages this morning. That's not too bad for a Monday morning.

7:05 a.m.: Rushing into Terminal 4, I make a beeline to British Airway's self check-in station. You must always use the self check-in station.

7:16 a.m.: Whew — close one. Running up to gate 47, I was distressed to see how eerily quiet the gate area was. Luckily, a flight attendant saw my frantic waving and kept the door open a few moments longer.

7:45 a.m.: Airborne after a slight air traffic delay, I seize a chance to crack open the laptop. Time to get focused on the day's work. I spend the body of the flight toggling back and forth on the pivot table in the Excel model — making changes to help clarify the statement of cash flows and head off potential ambiguities.

9:15 a.m.: "We are beginning our initial descent into Brussels." I wrap up my work and take a few moments to check my car rental reservations and confirm my schedule for the rest of the day. Unfortunately, since the client headquarters is in a far-off suburb of Brussels, a taxi trip is not an option. I count back the minutes from 1 p.m. With luck, I can be at the client site by 11 a.m. Just getting to the car rental pickup location could easily take 45 minutes.

9:57 a.m.: On the car rental shuttle bus with my early-morning adrenaline wearing off, I feel drowsy. Eyes shut, I ponder my decision to go home over the past weekend. My two colleagues on the engagement, Rolph and Jorge, elected to stay at the client site to work through the weekend. I went home, but now I'm regretting my decision.

10:12 a.m.: Finally on the road to ABC Pharmaceuticals after a quick car pickup at Europcar's Quick Pick-Up Aisle.

11:07 a.m.: Almost five hours after leaving home, I walk into conference room 52 A, the temporary location I have occupied the past few weeks. In the corner, Jorge, the BA-level research analyst assigned to this project, is typing feverishly on his computer — he doesn't even notice me enter.

Logging in to the client's network, I see to my dismay that 23 new emails have materialised. From the number of messages with "urgent" in the subject line, I gather that the morning has not gone well.

11:12 a.m.: Finally getting Jorge's attention and asking where Rolph is, I learn that Rolph has spent the morning shuttling from client manager to client manager, attempting to keep the project on track. Apparently, last week, M&A rumours surfaced in the industry, and now key managers in the operating division were questioning whether the organisational restructuring that we're working on is part of a broader plan to spin off the business unit.

11:17 a.m.: Still wondering where Rolph is, I open up the 58-slide PowerPoint presentation that they are set to review at 1 p.m. to begin making final edits and incorporating the updated Excel spreadsheets.

11:20 a.m.: Moments later, Rolph strides in — looking exasperated. "We need a major overhaul," he announces. Jorge and I exchange glances. "The division VP has had a change of heart — we need to adjust the restructuring plan." Listening intently as Rolph recaps the dozen conversations he's had throughout the morning, I flip through the

Visit **Vault Europe's Consulting Career Channel** at www.Vault.com/Europe for insider firm profiles, employee surveys of consultants in Europe, job listings, expert consulting career advice, insider salary information and more.

VAULT CAREER LIBRARY **157**

PowerPoint deck, reviewing the major sections and content of individual slides. Suddenly, an idea hits me. I outline a plan to revise the presentation, adding a brief new section in the beginning and moving most of the main body of the presentation to an appendix in the back. "Just what I was thinking," Rolph nods.

11:30 a.m.: Having divided the 58 slides into three parts, Rolph, Jorge and I "divide and conquer" to plough through the modifications they discussed. I take the largest section of slides — 30 in total, and am proud to set a pace of three minutes per slide for modifications.

1:00 p.m.: The 90 minutes have flown by, but the pieces are coming together. Rolph and Jorge are already in the meeting room, getting things started and passing out agendas. I cut and paste the last section of slides into my master deck. I send the deck to the assigned executive assistant for printing and photocopying.

1:15 p.m.: I step into the conference room, joining Rolph at the head of the table with the 15 client managers seated before them. Rolph has been in front of the group for 10 minutes, giving an overview of current status and buying time. I plug my laptop into the overhead projector just as the assistant distributes the photocopied handouts to the group.

1:17 p.m.: Stepping to the front of the room, I start my detailed discussion of the presentation slides. Dan is the primary "owner" of the deliverable. As the consultant who translates Rolph's direction into action and the person who directs Jorge's efforts — I am the "point person" for changes to the actual deliverable.

1:23 p.m.: Six minutes into my presentation, the first client manager interrupts to question the deliverable.

1:37 p.m.: Pushing through the presentation with a detailed knowledge of the material and client facilitation skills learned in the past few months, the meeting finally bogs down — what was intended as a "summary of deliverable" meeting has become a highly contentious work session. Faced with an increasing pace of client objections and new client information, I can only look to Rolph.

1:38 p.m.: Recognising the changed climate of the meeting, Rolph steps to the front to relieve me. After directing Jorge to grab a flip chart from the room next door, Rolph scrawls a new agenda with a magic marker.

3:55 p.m.: By now, all participants in the room realise that the entire scope of the project has changed — not just the specifics of the deliverable, but the project objectives, stakeholders, structure, and timetable. I discretely open my BlackBerry to begin to identify the ripple effect on my schedule for the rest of the week. No major crisis points, fortunately — but he will need to get in touch with the manager for my other project in London ASAP. It looks like I will be in Brussels for at least another two days this week.

4:15 p.m.: The meeting concludes, and Rolph, Jorge and I quickly excuse ourselves to check messages on e-mail and voice mail.

4:20 p.m.: I get on the phone with the firm's travel desk, cancelling the flight to London tonight and rescheduling for Thursday.

4:30 p.m.: I e-mail the London project manager, explaining the changes to the Brussels project and requesting advice on next steps. I then e-mail the firm's Research Network in Washington, following up on an earlier request for a dedicated researcher to analyse a client's survey results. I also send about a dozen other e-mails to colleagues to coordinate on other matters.

4:40 p.m.: Back in conference room 52A, Jorge is already typing up output from Rolph's flip charts. The next two hours are spent reviewing the outcome of the meeting, discussing necessary changes to the project timeline and deliverables, and prioritising next steps.

5:30 p.m.: Rolph suggests ordering some food. He needs to get to the airport for a flight to New York, to assist a partner on a business development proposal with a financial services firm located there. The first real meal of the day arrives at about 6:15 p.m. — I pick at the sushi absently as I stare at the financial model on my laptop.

7:30 p.m.: Feeling like the pharmaceutical client project's deliverables are under control for the time being, I check email again and messages again — several administrative items have popped up over the weekend and during the day. Having previously ignored them, I open up the messages partially for the relief of looking at something new. There's a request for feedback on my last project — an opportunity to provide 360 degree (upward) feedback on my last project manager. There is a reply from the Research Network group, providing a choice of several assistants for the London project. There is also an email from the SCG travel desk, confirming travel reservations for later in the week.

9:00 p.m.: Jorge gets up to pack up the laptop and go back to the hotel. Jorge and I chat briefly about the weekend and the hotel Rolph and Jorge are both staying at. I keep working, now turning my attention to reviewing data and project materials for the London project.

9:30 p.m.: The cleaning crew stops by, emptying the wastebaskets and spraying Lysol on the desks. I get a headache but continue to work.

Visit **Vault Europe's Consulting Career Channel** at **www.Vault.com/Europe** for insider firm profiles, employee surveys of consultants in Europe, job listings, expert consulting career advice, insider salary information and more.

VAULT CAREER LIBRARY **159**

10:15 p.m.: Feeling very tired now, I opt to pack it in. I get the rental car, and drive the five miles to the hotel.

11:00 p.m.: I call my girlfriend, set the alarm for 6:00 a.m. tomorrow and go to sleep.

IT Consultant

Kristine is a consultant at a major consulting firm with many IT consulting engagements. She graduated with a BA in Business Administration and has been with the company for four years. She's recently been staffed at a large telecommunications company. The company is revamping sales training. Her role is Team Lead of the design and developer for eight Web-based training modules. She has five analysts on her team.

4:30 a.m.: It's Monday morning. Time to wake up. There's time for a shower this Monday morning — such luxury!

5:30 a.m.: I am in a cab on the way to the airport, making a mental list of anything that could have been forgotten. I ask the cabbie to tune the radio to NPR.

6:10 a.m.: At the airport I go up to the self check-in kiosk. I take the boarding pass and head down to the security line, laptop and small carry-on in hand.

6:25 a.m.: At security, I remove my laptop from my bag and place it on the tray. I move through security quickly. No alarms beep.

6:35 a.m.: After a quick stop at Starbucks, I arrive at the gate. I say hello to three other members of my project and check out the other passengers I see every week on this Monday morning flight. I board early along with the other premier fliers — one of the perks of being a frequent traveller.

7:00 a.m.: The flight departs on time. Yay! I relish my window seat close to the front of the airplane.

8:00 a.m.: The beverage cart wakes me up. I ask for coffee and scan *The Financial Times* as I drink.

9:30 a.m.: I arrive at my destination and share a ride with my fellow consultants to the project site.

10:30 a.m.: At the project site. As I crawl underneath my desk to hook my laptop to the client LAN connection, one of my team members informs me that he still hasn't received feedback from his client reviewer. That's not good news.

11:00 a.m.: After checking and responding to e-mail, I call my team member's client reviewer. The reviewer agrees to send me the team member feedback on the training material by noon tomorrow.

Visit **Vault Europe's Consulting Career Channel** at **www.Vault.com/Europe** for insider firm profiles, employee surveys of consultants in Europe, job listings, expert consulting career advice, insider salary information and more.

VAULT   CAREER LIBRARY   **161**

11:15 a.m.: I remind the team of the 1 p.m. status meeting. I've got to start it on time — I have a meeting in town at 3:15 p.m. I start to review the content outlines for the training modules.

12:00 p.m.: I scurry, along with two team-mates, to get sandwiches at a nearby eatery. Mine is turkey and cheddar.

12:20 p.m.: Back at my desk, I get a call from the project manager, who is working at a client site in another state. He tells me that clients in the training department are nervous about their job security and asks that the entire team be sensitive to how the training changes may affect the training positions in the organisation.

1:00 p.m.: The team holds a status meeting. I pass on the message from the project manager. Each member discusses what has been completed and what he or she expects to complete that week. Two other team members are having difficulty obtaining feedback from their client reviewers. We all brainstorm ideas on how to obtain the feedback.

2:00 p.m.: I finish up the meeting and get directions to my meeting downtown.

2:40 p.m.: Off to the 3:15 p.m. meeting.

3:15 p.m.: I meet the head of the training department to discuss the training courses. He calls in a close associate who has opinions on how the courses should be organised. The associate wants to add several more Web-based training modules. I politely suggest that part of the additional subject matter could be covered in the modules that have been agreed to in the scope of the project. We all sketch out the course structure on a white board.

4:45 p.m.: Back at the project site. I check in with my team members via e-mail.

5:45 p.m.: I complete a draft of the course flow in PowerPoint and send it to the client and my manager for review.

7:00 p.m.: I have reviewed 50 percent of the course outlines. It's time to head back to the hotel. I stop by a local diner for a quick dinner.

8:30 p.m.: Time for a workout in the hotel gym.

9:15 p.m.: I'm ready for bed. Clothes for the next day are hanging in the closet. The alarm clock is set to 6:30 a.m.

10:30 p.m.: I go to sleep.

APPENDIX

Industry Buzzwords

About the Authors

CONSULTING

Industry Buzzwords

Balanced Scorecard

Balanced Scorecard defines what management means by "performance" and measures whether management is achieving desired results. The Balanced Scorecard translates Mission and Vision Statements into a comprehensive set of objectives and performance measures that can be quantified and appraised. These measures typically include the following categories of performance:

- Financial performance (revenues, earnings, return on capital, cash flow);
- Customer value performance (market share, customer satisfaction measures, customer loyalty);
- Internal business process performance (productivity rates, quality measures, timeliness);
- Innovation performance (percent of revenue from new products, employee suggestions, rate of improvement index);
- Employee performance (morale, knowledge, turnover, use of best demonstrated practices).

Boiling the ocean

Boiling the ocean is what consultants call over-analysis. In many consulting cases you will receive large amounts of information and inputs. It is within the job description of a good consultant to differentiate between interesting and superfluous information while always keeping the final objective in mind. No need to boil the ocean to make a cup of tea!

Business process reengineering

Business process reengineering involves the radical redesign of core business processes to achieve dramatic improvements in productivity, cycle times and quality. In business process reengineering, companies start with a blank sheet of paper and rethink existing processes to deliver more value to the customer. They typically adopt a new value system that places increased emphasis on customer needs. Companies reduce organizational layers and eliminate unproductive activities in two key areas. First, they redesign functional organizations into cross-functional teams. Second, they use technology to improve data dissemination and decision making.

Visit **Vault Europe's Consulting Career Channel** at www.Vault.com/Europe for insider firm profiles, employee surveys of consultants in Europe, job listings, expert consulting career advice, insider salary information and more.

VAULT CAREER LIBRARY 165

Change management

Change is a necessity for most companies if they are to grow and prosper. However, a recent study found that 70 percent of change programs fail. Change Management Programs are special processes executives deploy to infuse change initiatives into an organization. These programs involve devising change initiatives, generating organizational buy-in and implementing the initiatives as seamlessly as possible. Even armed with the brightest ideas for change, managers can experience difficulty convincing others of the value of embracing new ways of thinking and operating. Executives must rally firm-wide support for their initiatives and create an environment where employees can efficiently drive the new ideas to fruition.

Commercial due diligence

Commercial due diligence informs the funding process and enables clients to answer the fundamental question: "Are the commercial risks we intend to take understood, and will we get the returns that we require given the price we intend to pay." Due diligence analyses cover the macro market environment, the sectors in which the business is competing, the competitive environment faced, and the views and perceptions of current, former and potential customers of the business. Primary and secondary sources are used to evaluate pricing strategy, margin and volume information and a coherent view about the achievability of the business plan is developed.

Core competencies

A core competency is a deep proficiency that enables a company to deliver unique value to customers. It embodies an organization's collective learning, particularly of how to coordinate diverse production skills and integrate multiple technologies. Such a core competency creates sustainable competitive advantage for a company and helps it branch into a wide variety of related markets. Core Competencies also contribute substantially to the benefits a company's products offer customers. The litmus test of a Core Competency? It's hard for competitors to copy or procure. Understanding Core Competencies allows companies to invest in the strengths that differentiate them and set strategies that unify their entire organization.

Customer relationship management (CRM)

Customer relationship management (CRM) is a process companies use to understand their customer groups and respond quickly-and at times, instantly-to shifting customer desires. CRM technology allows firms to collect and manage large amounts of customer data and then carry out strategies based on that information. Data collected through focused CRM initiatives help firms solve specific problems throughout their customer relationship cycle- the chain of activities from the initial targeting of customers to efforts to win them back for more. CRM data also provide companies with important new insights into customers' needs and behaviors, allowing them to tailor products to targeted customer segments. Information gathered through CRM programs often generates solutions to problems outside a company's marketing functions, such as supply chain management and new product development.

Economic Value Added (EVA) analysis

Economic Value Added (EVA) analysis measures the amount of value a company has created for its shareholders. It determines how much profit a company has produced after it has covered the cost of its capital. Whereas conventional accounting methods deduct interest payments on debt, Economic Value Added analysis also deducts the cost of equity- what shareholders would have earned in price appreciation and dividends by investing in a portfolio of companies with similar risk profiles. EVA analysis thus offers a truer picture of the return a company delivers to its shareholders and provides a framework to assess options for increasing it. By making the cost of capital visible, EVA analysis helps companies identify whether they need to operate more efficiently, to focus investment on projects that are in the best interests of shareholders and to work to dispose of or reduce investment in activities that generate low returns.

80-20 approach

Consultants are often experts in prioritising and increasing effectiveness and the 80-20 approach is all about that. The theory is that a lot of effectiveness is lost by going into too much detail or that in order to achieve the 80% of the value only 20% of the time is needed and that the last 20% of value is gained in a gruesome 80% of the time. Since consulting work is often not so much about accuracy but more about broad overview, this theory is commonly applied.

KPI

KPI is short for 'key performance indicator' and is often used by companies to measure performance across all of their activities and processes. Consultants are often called in to help assess a company and come up with relevant KPIs. In the case of IT and process consultancies the KPIs are often part of the implementation process and seen as an important part of the ongoing monitoring. KPIs can also be used to measure success and can be built into the fees if using the 'pay for performance' model.

Visit **Vault Europe's Consulting Career Channel** at **www.Vault.com/Europe** for insider firm profiles, employee surveys of consultants in Europe, job listings, expert consulting career advice, insider salary information and more.

VAULT   CAREER LIBRARY   **167**

Matrix organisation

Larger consulting houses will often categorise their consultants by the means of a matrix. In the case of strategic consulting one of the axes of the matrix may be an industry (like consumer goods, capital goods, etc.), the other a set of skills (like pricing strategy, market entry strategy, etc.). A consultant will normally be placed somewhere on the matrix according to past work experience or projects and will be the primary choice when a case within his or her range of expertise comes up.

Out-of-the box thinking

A term often used by consultants to describe the ability to think beyond set patterns and borders (hence box). As you will know by now, consultants are often drafted in to assess problems, offer solutions and provide an external opinion. In all cases the unbiased approach and the ability to apply ideas used in other industries are a key contribution.

Supply chain management

Supply chain management synchronizes the efforts of all parties-suppliers, manufacturers, distributors, dealers, customers, etc.-involved in meeting a customer's needs. The approach often relies on technology to enable seamless exchanges of information, goods and services across organizational boundaries. It forges much closer relationships among all links in the value chain in order to deliver the right products to the right places at the right times for the right costs. The goal is to establish such strong bonds of communication and trust among all parties that they can effectively function as one unit, fully aligned to streamline business processes and achieve total customer satisfaction.

Total Quality Management (TQM)

Total Quality Management (TQM) is a systematic approach to quality improvement that marries product and service specifications to customer performance. TQM then aims to produce these specifications with zero defects. This creates a virtuous cycle of continuous improvement that boosts production, customer satisfaction and profits.

About the Authors

Jim Slepicka: Jim's career as a "creative problem-solver" began early, trouble-shooting operational challenges on the family farm. A strong believer in combining hands-on, practical experience with theoretical academic training, Jim ran his own business during high school and worked aboard for a year during college, traveling throughout Central & Eastern Europe and assisting the Czech Royal Family on consolidation of assets restituted after the Velvet Revolution (including several castles, a winery, brewery, spa and mineral water company).

Maintaining a focus on market-strategy issues, Jim's consulting experience has included roles with The Aberdeen Group, BP-Amoco Corporation, and most recently, PricewaterhouseCoopers' Strategic Change practice.

Jim is currently Co-Founder and President of Product Animations, Inc. and is a graduate of Harvard University and University of Chicago, Graduate School of Business.

Eric Chung: Having spent his childhood as a quant jock and later as a theoretical physics major in college, Eric is now applying his analytical skills to a career in consulting. Chung spent three years at Goldman Sachs, where he developed proprietary accounting and financial management systems for the firm. During business school, Eric was active in the management consulting group and was selected to teach a full-quarter class on leadership and communication skills to first-year students.

After spending a summer during business school interning at Accenture, he is currently a consultant with Strategic Decisions Group, a boutique firm specializing in decision making under uncertainty. He is also an active violinist, singer, songwriter, and director of a cappella singing groups. Chung is a graduate of Harvard College and the University of Chicago Graduate School of Business.

Philip Herrey: Philip spent his schooling and university years in Berlin, Massachusetts, Paris, New York, Shanghai and London. He has an MSc from the London School of Economics, spent eight years working for boutique consulting firms, focussing on consumer goods and retail, and has recently joined Roland Berger's UK practice as a project manager. Philip has completed the Executive MBA programme at London Business School.

Eduardo Junco: Eduardo has degrees in economics and engineering from the University of Cologne in Germany and Kings College in London. He currently lives

Visit **Vault Europe's Consulting Career Channel** at www.Vault.com/Europe for insider firm profiles, employee surveys of consultants in Europe, job listings, expert consulting career advice, insider salary information and more.

VAULT CAREER LIBRARY 169

in London, where he is a PMSI consultant specialising in the alchoholic beverage market as well as the fields of commercial due diligences for private equity funds.

As a responsible publishing company, Vault is proud to work with printers who source materials from well managed sustainable forests: this ensures long term timber supplies and helps protect the environment.

We aim to grow our business while minimizing our impact on the environment.

We encourage readers to download and read the electronic versions of our guides available on our web sites, www.vault.com and www.vault.com/europe.

We are also proud to have installed the Vault Online Career Library at 850 universities worldwide. With the Online Career Library, students worldwide can download electronic versions of our guides as part of their job search preparation. By providing this service to students, Vault and its university partners help reduce the printing and shipping of our guides

By leveraging the latest technology, we aim to contribute responsibly to the world in which we live.

Thomas Nutt
General Manager
Vault Europe